Aditya Behl was born in Jabalpur (Madhya Pradesh) in 1966, and received his early education in India. He read classics at Bowdoin College of Brunswick, Maine, and is currently completing a doctorate in the History of Religions at the University of Chicago. His intellectual interests are in comparative religions and literary theory, and he writes on Hindi Sufi romances and Indian cultural history. He has translated fiction and poetry from Hindi, Urdu, and Punjabi into English, and is currently translating the work of Krishna Sobti for Penguin India.

David Nicholls has been editor of *Chicago Review* since 1991. He was born and raised in Indianapolis, Indiana, where he graduated from Brebeuf Preparatory School in 1984. In 1988, he received his AB in English and philosophy from Bowdoin College of Brunswick, Maine. He earned an MA in English from the University of Chicago in 1989. He has been a Jacob K. Javits National Graduate Fellow from 1989–1993, and is most recently the recipient of a Mellon Dissertation Fellowship. In 1994, he will receive a Ph.D. in English Language and Literature from the University of Chicago. He is currently working on a book, *Conjuring the Folk: Modernity, Folk Aesthetics, and African-American Narrative, 1915–1945*.

The Penguin New Writing in India

Edited by

Aditya Behl and David Nicholls

PENGUIN BOOKS

Penguin Books India (P) Ltd., 210, 43 Chiranjiv Tower, Nehru Place, New Delhi 110 019, India
Penguin Books Ltd., 27 Wrights Lane, London W8 5TZ, UK
Penguin Books USA Inc., 375 Hudson Street, New York, NY 10014, USA
Penguin Books Australia Ltd., Ringwood, Victoria, Australia
Penguin Books Canada Ltd., 10 Alcorn Avenue, Suite 300, Toronto, Ontario M4V 3B2, Canada
Penguin Books (NZ) Ltd., 182-190 Wairau Road, Auckland 10, New Zealand

First published by *Chicago Review* (Volume 38, Numbers 1 & 2) 1992
Revised and published as *The Penguin New Writing in India* by Penguin Books India (P) Ltd. 1994

Copyright © *Chicago Review* 1992

10 9 8 7 6 5 4 3 2 1
The cover shows a painting titled "Chase" by A. Ramachandran
Courtesy: CIMA
Cover design by Sunil Sil

Typeset in Palatino by Digital Technologies and Printing Solutions, New Delhi

The following poems will be reprinted in Vinay Dharwadker and A.K. Ramanujan, eds., *Modern Indian Poetry: An Anthology* [forthcoming, OUP & University of California Press]—"Poem" by Pratibha Nandkumar; "Electric Lights Come to Puttalli" by H.S. Venkateshamurthy; "Avatars" by V. Indira Bhavani; "White Paper" by Nara; "American Tourist" by B.C. Ramachandra Sharma; and "To Mother" by S. Usha.
The following poems are from Arlene R.K. Zide, ed., *In Their Own Voice: The Penguin Anthology of Contemporary Indian Women Poets* (Penguin India, 1993)—"Poem" by Pratibha Nandkumar; "Wanted: A Broom" by Chandrakanti; "Two Women Knitting" by Mrinal Pande; "The Night Has Come To An End" by Aruna Dhere; "One After Another After Another" by Teji Grover; "The Girl's Desire Moves Among The Bangles" by Gagan Gill; "Along The Railroad Track" by Kanchan Kuntala Mukherjee; "Street Dog" by Amrita Pritam; "The Slant" by Savitri Rajeevan; "To Mother" by S. Usha; "The Tryst" by Sunanda Tripathy; and "Avatars" by V. Indira Bhavani

In Memoriam
A. K. Ramanujan
1929–1993

Contents

Introduction

This anthology is designed to introduce the English language reader to the extraordinary range of contemporary Indian writing. In recent years, Indian writers have enjoyed unprecedented international interest: Vikram Seth, Bharati Mukherjee, Salman Rushdie and others have captured the attention of readers worldwide. Originally published as a special issue of *Chicago Review*, this collection presents a way into the multiple literary communities operating in India today, communities whose work often goes unnoticed in an international marketplace preoccupied with the literary blockbuster. The book shares the editorial logics of two different forms of literary assemblage, the literary magazine and the anthology: we sought both to present fresh new works and to provide a sense of historical and linguistic balance, so as to convey new developments along with ongoing traditions in Indian writing. The result is a book that will provide an excellent introduction for the reader new to Indian literatures, while also providing many surprises for the initiated.

Representing a subcontinent like India between the covers of a single book involves many difficulties, both logistical and intellectual. The literary scene in a multilingual society presents the editor with a bewildering variety of literary talents working in many dialects and languages. This necessitates putting together a collection which is largely 'literature-in-translation', that problem category for editors who have multilingual fields to cover. As we put together a range of translations which show the relations between genres, languages, and literary movements in more than a dozen languages, and literary movements in more than a dozen languages, we encountered two intellectual problems inherent to the project of producing an anthology of Indian literature. First, the colonialists and nationalists invention of Indian literature produces an idea of coherence and unity that is unwarranted. The Indian literary canon is not a fixed tradition unfolding uniformly across time, but is rather made up of multiple cultural practices and temporalities. Second, at a time when the practice of translation is under ideological scrutiny, we had to consider the political effects of rendering our multilingual field as seemingly transparent to the English-language reader. Here, we want to come to the defense of translation: translations make possible the critical discussion of texts, literary movements, and cultural phenomena which has been multilingual and multiliterate for centuries, translations are a necessary component of social interaction. This anthology is a modest attempt to map an India whose literary scene is vital, diverse, and changing.

A survey of the table of contents suggests the variety of languages and cultural perspectives brought together here. Works from thirteen languages are included in this issue: Bengali, English, Gujarati, Hindi, Kannada, Malayalam, Marathi, Oriya, Punjabi, Sindhi, Tamil, Telugu, and Urdu. Authors from several literary movements, including the Progressives of the 1930s and the movement for new poetry, are represented generously in these pages. Women writers comprise about half the contributors here, ranging from Mahadevi Varma, whose 1934 essay is considered a classic of Indian feminism, through the 1960s to the present. A number of our writers are expatriates, living in the United States and Britain, and their work often reflects on life in the Indian diaspora. Vinay Dharwadker's essay, "Some Contexts of Modern Indian Poetry," brings the collection to a close, and we direct you there and to the notes on contributors for help in placing these authors regionally and historically.

We hope that English-language readers will take up this book's invitation to read more widely in Indian literatures. Given the current political climate, there is a considerable need to extend cross-cultural understanding. We think this book will provide many insights into the multiple points of view and modes of cultural expression current in today's India.

Many people contributed to the creation of this book, not least of whom are the writers and translators whose efforts fill these pages. During the process of selection, William Douglas helped us to read and to evaluate the hundreds of manuscripts we had to consider. Angela Sorby provided assistance in her role as managing editor at the Chicago Review office. Chicago Review is supported by the Division of the Humanities at the University of Chicago, and we are grateful to Connie Cheung and John Whaley of the Dean of Humanities office for their continued assistance. We received valuable help in the gathering of material from Rimli Bhattacharya, David Davidar, Kamalini Dutt, Sharon Lowen, C.M. Naim, the late A.K. Ramanujan, D.S. Rao and the staff of the Sahitya Akademi, the late Raghuvir Sahay, and Arlene R.K. Zide. Finally, we are deeply grateful to the Witter Bynner Foundation for a Process of Translation Grant; this book would not have been possible without their generous support.

Chicago   *Aditya Behl & David Nicholls*
1 March 1994

Poem

When I was groping for a new poem
for the poetry festival,
poems danced all over the house:
in nooks and corners, in the bed,
in boxes, in walls and curtains,
in windows and doors
poems beckoned with their hands.
They simmered on the stove
in the rasam pot, got flattened
under the rolling-pins
on the chapatti stone,
and diced on the knife-stand
they boiled in the cooker
with salt and spices,
sautéed, smelling fragrant.

In the hall they were lying about
begging to be picked up.
If I swept them, they asked
to be mopped; if I mopped them,
they wanted to be dressed,
stubborn pests, thorns
in my flesh.
Curtains where little hands
had wiped themselves,
torn books, sandals dropped,
chairs and tables pulled here and there,

clothes strewn on the floor
took on the shapes of poems
and dazzled my eyes.
When I cleared the mess
and sat down to rest,
one of them pestered me
asking me now to wash it,
now to give it a drink,
now to come play with it.

When at last I sat down to write
not one letter got written
and my brain was in a fog.
Late at night, when a sleepy hand
groped and hugged me,
'To hell with the poem,' I said
and fell asleep.
But it tickled me in a dream,
made me laugh and charmed me.

When I read that
in the poetry festival,
it ran out, refused to come back,
went inside the listeners and sat there.
I let it sit there
and came home alone.

Translated from the Kannada by A. K. Ramanujan

Desert Rose

All the seven skies
are broken
a bright wind seals
the infant's mouth

Sand dunes reap
the pillaged city
the vine bears
fruit

Colossal grapes
of rock
black rock
to have

Or hold
at heart
the driven self
near sightless

As hands
split bread
and strip
the desert rose.

Estrangement becomes the mark of the eagle

I

We lie in a white room, on a bed with many pillows
next to a window just above a street

You whisper: exile is hard
let me into your mouth, let me blossom

I listen for I know the desert is all around
the muggers and looters, caravan men with masked faces
and Mesopotamia's largesse under tanks
and the colonels of Texas and Florida
with cockatoo feathers in their teeth
and the young lads of Oregon torn from their pillows
bent under bombs, grenades, gas masks
and the young lads of Kuwait beheaded in the sand.

II

Estrangement becomes the mark of the eagle
a signal corpus, bonanza of dew
the portals of paradise are sunk

Yet all that surrenders as we do, lover infant godhead,
nothing makes blank, nothing kills, not
the chill hauteur of elegies, not gunshot wounds

But vision clamps. Bloodied feathers
in a young woman's mouth, torn from a colonel's cap,
she spits them out, she comes from Tiruvella, my hometown
heart undercover, belly huge in desert sand she squats
by the barbed wire of a transit camp outside Amman

Behind her back a ziggurat of neon
marking the eagle's pure ascent
in whose aftermath small bodies puff with ash.

III

We lie in a white room, on a bed with many pillows
just above the street, the world's a blackened market-place

No codicil: *Mujh-se pahli-si muhabbat. . .** dearest heart
I can no longer repeat the rest of that.

Where we are, a child, her jeans filled with blood,
gags on dropped vegetables, half-cooked rice
she picked up as she knelt in the trash.
Below her, smashed subway cars imported from Japan
crumple thirty feet down underneath our gate

While men well trained to the purchase of power
knot water bottles, burst cans of shaving cream
spent condoms, to the rear ends of jeeps and race
at the crack of dawn, at the bitten end of our century
through Broadway, through narrow desert tracks.

---

* The entire line runs: *'Mujh-se pahli-si muhabbat, meri mahbub, na mang.'* It is the first
line of the celebrated poem by Faiz Ahmed Faiz and in translation may be
rendered as: 'Beloved, do not ask me for that love again.'

Gulam mohammed Sheikh

Returning Home

In the afternoon when everyone was resting I would go to *dada's**
old room and sit there by myself. Sometimes I would write odd
scraps or make pictures. In the midst of this activity there would
be several pauses, during which my gaze would slowly fix itself
on the wall rising outside the door. The top of the wall stayed
outside the frame, but I could see the edge hard and clear along the
ground. For years I had observed it with great curiosity, as it
separated our lane from the mill compound. One end of the wall
joined up with the houses in the crowded section of the town, the
other sank into the warm belly of the dry river bed; about
twenty-five feet high and five hundred feet long, this wall has split
my child's world neatly into two—one world lies on this side, the
other across it. My childhood belongs to the small universe that lies
on the side where we stand; that beyond is still unfamiliar to me.

I have watched this wall with a hypnotic fascination for so long
now that the yellow stones, markings on the mortar, the rough
pattern of the surface have all come to lodge within my mind.
Against these stones, we would mark off our height in notches on
the wall, and our games and races were measured off against its
length. In our vivid imagination, this was the most invincible
curiosity in the world. We had never really had the opportunity to
scale it or look beyond it. Flying kites, we would clamber up on the
roof and stand on the tips of our toes to try and look at what lay
beyond, but saw nothing except the chimneys of the mill and a few
desultory rooftops. There was nothing exceptional beyond, but the

---

* Dada: grandfather

wall held our minds so fiercely captive that we imagined it to be a sacred serpent guarding a wonderful treasure, and had no intention of confronting reality as it was.

Sometimes we thought we saw a small depression in the wall, and taking a pebble would try to file a tiny hole inwards; working the stone absently into the dent the mind would begin to wander and I would find myself scratching my name in rounds about it. Sitting on the threshold of *dada's* room, I would confront the stoutness of the wall; staring resolutely at it I would bore a clear, minuscule opening through it. Occasionally I would, from staring, become mesmerized and fall into a half-reverie, and my drowsy glances hopped and slid over its heavy-grained surface. The transforming afternoon sun would cast long scratches on its rough face; sometimes, I saw wonderful shapes on its surface, and the wall appeared momentarily to be transparent. When the shadows changed we would be left with a great sense of loss. Along with my childhood this wall is etched so deep in my being that today, seeing a lonely fort or ruined enclosure is to draw a similar emotion from it, and looking at a fragment of masonry in a bereft ruin at Mandu the mind becomes still; its loneliness still rambles through my thoughts. This strange isolation is still a link to my childhood. Within the house the bricks encircle a body of space that lives. This lifeless wall stretches along like a line without soul or form. Its existence is confined to its strange ability to divide the land it stands on.

With the rising and setting of the sun the cordon of the wall kept changing. With the light of early morning, when its shadow fell on the entrance to *dada's* room, until the afternoon, this shadow would stretch along thinly like a veil. At midday the slim dark line of the shadow would lie along the ground at the bottom of the wall like a mysterious scarf, and the dogs would come sniffing and try to pull at it with their teeth. Sitting in the doorway, I would enjoy the sensation of the shadow passing slowly over my body. Resting in the slow edges of this passing shade, I would feel for a moment that I actually touched the wall.

Remembering the wall now I remember too the faces I have seen before it. Endlessly, for years, the eyes and voices of these people have fought its unrelenting visage. The ear-splitting screaming of the mill-worker's widow, the bawling of the drunk Allahrakha, Ahmadchacha's twenty-five-year-old vigil for a long-lost cousin not yet returned from Africa, sitting still by the wall with his two unmarried sons who'd squandered the years, their lives. As though reflecting something of the stones in the wall, their very forms change, their voices become listless. My own home has not been spared this transforming experience; watching my mother's wrinkled countenance, a silent fear comes over me as I think of the wall that has gouged its own markings so clearly on her face.

The years still nestle in the deep of this wall. It knows neither night nor day; and although time keeps loosening its rocks, persistently shedding grainy pebbles from its scaly surface, it has not yet succeeded in boring even the tiniest hole through it.

Translated from the Gujarati by Mala Marwah
using the author's Hindi version

Room

These days the sun seems to come again
            from somewhere
into my corner room. As if from somewhere
            sun, rain,
nocturnal dewfall, everything comes in
            just as before;
the eyes go blind in dust-storms.
Varied patterns of lines appear once more,
            from stains of salt rot
on the northern wall. These days, again somehow
all that whitewash, all those repairs
have grown irrelevant, like the old days;
the room gets wet again in the pouring rain,
            the floor
cracks open in mid-summer noon. Again,
just as before, the eyes in the dust-storm
go blind inside the room.

Translated from the Bengali by Sunil B. Ray and Carolyne Wright
with the poet

So Many Crazy Blue Hills

All the blue hills fade out slowly
under the advancing wall,
and suddenly
a naked tree looms out in front
incredibly clear.
The incongruous flame of a muffled sun
suddenly dolls him up
almost ludicrous,
the bony arms get all entangled
by the grace of light ripping through the screen,
exposing him secretly busy with his private affairs.
He looks powerful, terrifying, many-armed,
like the copper image of a naked god.
The mottled background gradually loses itself
under a thick white coating.
Every wave of white has a pure gold border
on the slope of every hill.
The tall tower holds in its grasp
whatever there is to hold. As if at
        the summit's window
a fire breaks out, a small tongue of flame
dances on the summit's cone, like
a bad angel wrapped in a halo.

And
under reddish roofs, white cottages
grow indolent, weary, pregnant;
then
clouds change their tunes, then
lights change their dance, then
all the blue hills are born again
from empty space.

Translated from the Bengali by Sunil B. Ray and Carolyne Wright
with the poet

The Five-Dollar Smile

'Make this child smile again,' the black type on the crumpled, glossy news weekly page read. 'All it takes is five dollars a month.'

Joseph stared at the picture sandwiched between the two halves of the caption. He had seen it a thousand times—the tattered clothes, the dark, intense, pleading eyes, the grubby little fingers thrust tightly into a sullenly closed mouth. The photo that had launched the most successful, worldwide appeal in HELP's history, four years ago. His picture.

As usual, he viewed it once more with that curious detachment that had come to him during those last four years. He could not see it as a photograph of himself, a record of his past, a souvenir of his younger childhood. It was not personal enough for that; it was in the public domain, part of an advertisement, a poster, a campaign, and now an ageing magazine clipping in his hand. The little boy who stared out at him was not him, Joseph Kumaran; he was part of a message, defined by a slogan, serving a purpose, and the fact that he was Joseph Kumaran did not matter. It never had.

Joseph looked once more at the picture, as he had five times already during the flight, as if to reassure himself that he knew what he was doing on this large, cold, humming monster hurtling him towards a strange land he had known only in postage stamps. That's what this is all about, he wanted the picture to say. That's who you are and the reason why you are on an unfamiliar thing called an aeroplane and why your feet don't touch the ground but your toes feel cold and you have to put a belt around your waist that stops you from leaning forward comfortably to eat the strange food they expect you to get at with plastic forks and knives, sealed impossibly in polythene, while you wish you could pluck up the nerve to ask the poised, distant and impossibly tall, white lady to help you, help you with a blanket and two pillows and some real food you can eat without trying to gnaw at sealed packages of cutlery . . .

He folded the picture again and pushed it into the pocket of the tight little blazer he had been given the day he left the HELP office with Sister Celine to go to the airport. It had been sent with a bundle of old clothes for the disaster relief collection, he had learned, and though it was a little small for him it was just the thing to smarten him up for the trip to the United States. Always be smart, Joseph,' Sister Celine had said. 'Let them know you're poor but you're smart, because we knew how to bring you up.

Joseph sat back, his feet dangling from the aeroplane seat, and looked at the largely uneaten food on the tray. When he thought of food he could remember the day of the photograph. He had been seven then: that was the day he had learned he was seven.

'How old's that little kid? The one in the torn white shirt?'

'He's about seven. No one s really sure. He came here when he was a little child. We couldn't really tell when he'd been born.'

'About seven, eh. Looks younger *click, whirr.* 'Might be what I'm looking for. Get him away from that food Sister will you please? We want a hungry child not a feeding one.

Suddenly, a large white hand interposed among the tiny outstretched brown ones crowded at the table, pulling Joseph s away. 'Come here, Joseph. This nice man wants to see you.

'But I want to eat Sister. Desperation, pleading in his voice. He knew what could happen if he was too late. There would be no food left for him: it had happened before. And today was his favourite day, with crisp *papadams* in the *kanji* gruel. He had watched the cooks rip up and fry the *papadams* from behind the kitchen door, and he'd tried to get to the table early so he wouldn't miss out on his share. He'd had to fight the bigger boys to stay there, too. But what determined resistance had preserved, Sister Celine was taking away.

'Please, Sister, please.

'Later, child. Now behave yourself.' He was dragging his feet and she was pulling him quite firmly by the left hand. 'And if you don't walk properly I shall have to take the cane to you.' He straightened up quickly; he knew the cane well and did not want it again.

Would the air-hostess take a cane to him if he asked her for a fork and knife? Of course she wouldn't, he knew that. He knew his nervousness was silly, unnecessary. He was suddenly hungry, but he didn't know how to attract her attention. She was giving a man a drink several rows in front of Joseph.

'Miss!' he called softly. His voice came out huskily, tripping over dry obstacles in his throat. She didn't hear him; he wished desperately that she would catch his eye, and he trained his look on her with such fearful intensity it was unbelievable she should not notice. 'Miss!' he called again, waving his hand. She was sticking a pin into the headrest of the man who'd bought the drink, and she still didn't hear.

'Miss!' This time it was too loud. It seemed to Joseph that everyone in the plane had turned to look at him, as if he had done something very odd. There were a couple of smiles, but for the most part people looked disapproving, frowning their displeasure at him and making comments to their neighbours. Joseph's dark cheeks flushed red with embarrassment.

The air-hostess straightened up, controlled her irritation, and smiled sweetly but briskly as she walked down to him.

'Can-I-have-a-knife-and-fork-please?' The words came out in a rush, Sister Angela's diction lessons forgotten in his anxiety.

She hardly seemed to pause in her stride. 'It's on your tray—here, on the side, see? In this packet.' And she lifted the packet, placed it on top of the napkin for him to see, and before he could say anything more, strode off down the aisle.

'Hold it there, kid.' Joseph, seven, wanting *papadams*, confronted American slang for the first time in the person of a large, white man with a moustache and a camera. To little Joseph, everything seemed large about the man: his body, his moustache, his camera. A large hand pushed him back a little and a voice boomed: 'Seems rather small for his age.'

'Infant malnutrition. Mother died in childbirth and his father brought him through the forest alone. These tribals are astonishingly hardy. God knows how he survived without any

14

permanent damage.'

'So there's nothing really wrong with him, right? I mean, his brain's okay and everything? I've gotta be sure I'm selling the American public poverty and not retardation, if you see what I mean. So he's normal, huh?'

'Just a little stunted.' Sister Celine, quiet, precise. *Click, whirr.* Lights exploded at him. His eyes widened.

'Let's take him outside, if you don't mind. I'd like to use the sun—I'm not too sure of my flash.'

'Yes, of course, Mr Cleaver. Come, Joseph.'

He squirmed out of the nun's grasp. 'But, Sister, I want to eat.'

'Later. Now if you're difficult there'll be no lunch at all for you.'

Resentfully, he followed them out into the courtyard. He stood there sullenly, staring his quiet hatred at the large man. *Click, whirr, click.* 'Move him to this side a bit, won't you, Sister?'

It was being pushed around that made him thrust his fingers into his mouth, as much in self-protection as in appeasement of his palate. The photographer clicked again.

Joseph turned to look at the air-hostess' retreating back in profound dismay. Why hadn't he told her that he knew he had a knife and fork, but he didn't know how to get at them? Why hadn't he made clear what exactly was the help he needed? Why had he been so scared?

He drew himself even more deeply into his seat and looked around nervously. His neighbour, staring out of the window, smiled briefly, mechanically at him. Joseph could not ask him to help. Or could he? The man turned from the window to a magazine he was reading over dinner. Joseph's resolution faded.

That day, after the photographs, there had been no *papadams* left for him. Only cold *kanji*; the *papadams* were already finished.

'See—I told you you could have lunch later,' the nun said. 'Here's your lunch now.'

But I wanted the *papadams*, he wanted to scream in rage and frustration. And why did you need to take me away from my *papadams*? What was so important about that man with the camera that you had to deprive me of something I've been waiting a month to enjoy? But he did not say all that. He could not. Instead, the lump

15

in his throat almost choking him, he flung the tin plate of gruel to the ground and burst into tears.

'Good heavens—what's the matter with him today? Very well, no lunch for you then, Joseph. And you will clean this mess off the floor and come to my office as soon as you have done so, so that you may be suitably punished for your ingratitude. There are many little boys not as fortunate as you are, Joseph Kumaran. And don't you forget it.'

Sniffing back his misery, Joseph knew he would not forget it. He would have six strokes of the cane to remember it by.

How could he ask his neighbour to help open the packet? He was so engrossed in his magazine. And he was eating. It seemed so wrong, and so embarrassing. Joseph tried to speak, but the words would not come out.

At the end of the aisle, another stewardess was already bringing tea or coffee around. The other passengers seemed to be finishing their meals. They would take his tray away from him and he would not even have eaten. A panic, irrational but intense, rose to flood him.

He struggled with the packet. He tried to tear it, gnaw at it, rip it open. It would not give way. The cutlery inside the packet jangled; at one point he hit a cup on his tray and nearly broke it. Joseph's attempts became even wilder and he made little noises of desperation.

'Here,' his neighbour's strong voice said. 'Let me help you.'

Joseph turned to him in gratitude. He had hoped his desperation would become apparent and attract assistance. It had worked.

'Thank you,' he managed to say. 'I didn't know how to open it.'

'It's quite easy,' his neighbour said.

The first copies of the photographs arrived at the HELP Centre a few weeks after the photographer had gone. Joseph had almost forgotten the incident, even the caning, though the frustration of the *papadam*-less gruel remained. One of the nuns called him to Sister Eva's office excitedly.

'Look, Joseph—these are the pictures the nice man took, the day you were so bad,' Sister Celine told him. 'This is you.'

16

Joseph looked at the black-and-white image without curiosity. He would rather not have seen it, rather not have been reminded of their perverse cruelty to him that day. He stared at the picture, made no comment and looked away.

'It's going to be used in a worldwide appeal.' Sister said. 'Your picture will be in every important magazine in the world. Helping us get money to help other children. Doesn't that make you happy, Joseph?'

He had learned to be dutiful. 'Yes, Sister,' he said.

The man in the seat next to him turned the polythene packet around, slipped out a flap and deftly extricated a fork and a knife. He handed them to Joseph with a cordial smile.

'There—you see, easy.'

'Thank you.' Joseph, taking the implements from the man, felt his ears burning with shame. So there had been no need to try and tear open the packet after all. There was a flap. He turned single-mindedly to the food, wanting to shut the rest of the world, witness to his humiliation, out of his sight and hearing.

The first MAKE THIS CHILD SMILE AGAIN poster was put up in the HELP office just behind Sister Eva's desk, so those who came in would be struck by it as soon as they entered and looked for her. It was put up without any fuss or ceremony, and Joseph only knew it was there because the door to Sister Eva's office had been open when he and a group of boys had been walking down the corridor to their daily classes. It was one of the other boys who had noticed it first and drawn everyone else's attention to it.

The slogan soon became a joke. 'Smile, Joseph, smile,' his friends would tease him. And if he was in a particularly angry mood, one of the boys would ask with mock gravity, 'Has anyone got five dollars?' Sometimes Joseph would only get angrier, but sometimes he would be provoked to smile at them. They used to call it 'the five-dollar smile.'

The food was terrible. It was totally unfamiliar to Joseph's taste buds, anyway, and he did not enjoy it. There was, however, a bowl of fruit salad on the tray that contained little diced apples. He ate those, spilling some on the seat and the floor. He did not know whether to be happy about the pieces he had eaten or sad about the ones he had lost. He looked around to see if anyone was watching him. No one was. He tried to pick up a little piece of apple from the floor but the tray was in his way and he couldn't reach down far enough. It was frustrating. On balance, he felt miserable.

The air-hostess swished by to collect his tray. Would he like some tea? Joseph said, 'Yes.' Actually he wanted coffee but he was scared that if he said 'no' to the tea he might not be offered any coffee either. Why couldn't they have offered him coffee first? he thought, as the pale, brown liquid filled his cup. It was so unfair.

He was, not surprisingly, the first child to be 'adopted'. Other people who responded to the campaign had sent in their five dollars for the first month, and their pledges for a year or two years or a decade or a lifetime, for any child HELP wanted to rescue. But three couples insisted their money go to one specific child—the child in the photograph. They had seen his sad, little face and they wanted to make him smile again. No one else. Their five dollars was for Joseph Kumaran's tiny little fingers to come out of his hungry little mouth. And they insisted on being allowed to adopt him alone.

The nuns had sighed when those letters came in. 'Oh, what a nuisance some people are,' Sister Eva said. 'I have half a mind to return their money to them. It's none of their business to tell us where their money should go.' But Sister Eva had kept the money and the pledges anyway—from all three couples. Joseph Kumaran's five-dollar smile was actually netting HELP fifteen dollars a month.

So every month Joseph would have to sit down and, in his neat, strained little hand, write a letter to each of his fosterparents, thousands of miles away, telling them how good and grateful he was. 'Today we had catechism and I learned the story of how Lot's wife turned into a banana tree,' he would write to one couple. (Salt was an expensive commodity in those parts and the nuns didn't want the children to derive the wrong lessons from the Bible.) Then he would copy the same line out neatly onto the other two letters. As he grew older, Sister Celine would no longer dictate the letters but let him write them himself and correct them before they were mailed. 'Sister Angela has told me about America,' he wrote once. 'Is it true that everyone is rich there and always has plenty to eat?' Sister Celine did not like that, scored it out and was later seen speaking sternly to Sister Angela.

The steward was coming down the aisle selling earphones. Joseph had seen him doing that as the flight began, and though he did not know what earphones were, he had discovered that they cost money and that people put them into their ears. He shook his head vigorously when asked whether he wanted one. But his anxious eyes rolled in curiosity as his neighbour, who had also declined the first time, looked at the movie handbill in approbation, produced green notes and silver coins and was rewarded with a polythene packet. From this emerged a contraption even stranger at close quarters than it had seemed from a distance.

The curtains were being drawn across the aeroplane windows; a screen was lowered at the head of the cabin; images flickered on the whiteness ahead. Joseph stared, transfixed, rapt. His neighbour had plugged in his earphone and was obviously listening to something Joseph could not hear. Titles began to appear on the screen.

Joseph desperately wanted to hear the movie, too.

He would get letters in reply from his fosterparents. Initially, they were as frequent as his monthly letters to them, but later their interest seemed to flag and he would get only occasional replies. One couple seemed the nicest—they would always apologize profusely whenever their letters were too late and they would always ask about him, his schoolwork, his games. On Christmas they would send little gifts that Sister Celine would let him open but which he would have to share with the other children. Joseph liked their coloured notepaper, the lady's handwriting, which was so easy to read, and the lingering smell of perfume that still clung to each sheet of stationery. Frequently he would hold it up to his face, smothering his nose in it, smelling America.

One day, after several letters to this couple, he became bolder. 'It is very hot here at this time of year,' he had written in the version approved by Sister Celine. 'I suppose it is cooler in America.' But while copying the corrected draft out neatly onto an aerogramme, he added: 'I think I would enjoy America very much.' He told no one about the addition, sealed the aerogramme and waited excitedly for a reply.

When it came, there was no reference to what he had written.

19

But Joseph did not give up. 'I often wonder whether America has trees like the ones in my drawing,' he hinted while enclosing a precocious crayon sketch. And in the next letter, 'If I came to America, do you think I might like it?' He was so enamoured of this approach that he copied that line into each of his three letters and sent them away.

It worked. His favourite 'parents', the ones who sent him Christmas presents, wrote to Sister Celine to say that they'd often wanted to see the little boy they'd 'adopted' but they'd never been able to manage a trip to India. Would it not be possible for young Joseph to be sent to America instead? As soon as they heard from Sister Celine, they would be happy to enclose an air-ticket for the little boy. Of course, they were not suggesting that he should stay with them always. Obviously, his place was amongst 'his people' in India and 'with you all at HELP'. They would send him back, but they did so want to see him, just once.

Sister Celine seemed a little taken aback by the letter. It was not customary for fosterparents to evince such an interest in their protégés. When they were old enough the children were simply taught an elementary trade and packed off to earn their keep. Foreign trips, for however short a duration, were highly unusual.

Sister Celine showed Joseph the letter and asked, 'You haven't been up to anything, have you?' To his excited protestations she merely responded, 'We'll see.' And then she went to talk to Sister Eva.

Joseph had only seen one movie before. That was a document-ary about HELP's activities among orphan children in the wilds of Bihar, and it had been shown one evening after dinner by the man who made it, so that the nuns could all see what the outside world was being told about their work. Sister Eva, in a spirit of generosity, had suggested that the boys, at least those over five, be permitted to sit on the ground and watch it too. It might teach them a few things, she told the other nuns, make them realize how much we do for them, maybe instil some gratitude in them. Joseph had fallen asleep halfway through that movie. He didn't want to see starving Adivasi children and warm-hearted nuns; he saw them every day. The black-and-white images, the monotonous, superimposed voice of the commentator, blurred in his mind; the nuns danced tiptoe through the crevices of his brain, and the pictures pulsed and faded in his eyes. Firm but gentle hands were rousing him.

'Get up—it's time to go to bed.'

In the background, Sister Eva's high-pitched voice rang through the clear night: 'Look at them! Give them a special treat like this and half of them go off to sleep! Don't ever let me catch any of you asking to see a movie again. I mean it!'

But what a movie this was. Bright, vivid colours, pretty, white women in short dresses, fast cars racing down broad, foreign streets. It was like nothing he had ever seen before. And he wanted to hear it; hear the loud roar of the car engines, the soft, tinkling laughter of the women, the shouts and the screams and all the sound of bullets and people and whizzing aeroplanes.

'Sir.' The steward who had dispensed the earphones was standing at the end of the aisle, just behind Joseph, watching the movie too.

'Yes?'

'May I have some earphones too?'

'Of course.' The steward disappeared behind the partition and emerged with a polythene packet. He handed it to Joseph.

Joseph reached out to take it with an ineffable feeling of awe, wonder and achievement. He pushed aside the flap, put in his hand and touched the cold plastic. The sensation was indescribably thrilling.

'Two dollars and fifty cents, please.'

'But ... but ... I don't have any money,' Joseph said miserably. His eyes pleaded with the steward. 'Please?'

The steward had a why-are-you-wasting-my-time-you-dumb-child look on his face. 'I'm sorry,' he said, taking the packet out of Joseph's hands, 'IATA regulations.'

And then he was gone, having invoked an authority higher than Joseph's longings, more powerful than philanthropy. When he re-emerged from the partition it was on the other side, on the aisle away from Joseph's.

Sister Eva had taken some time to decide. It was not that she minded in principle, she told Sister Celine, that this could set a dangerous precedent. The other children would be wanting to go too, and how many had rich American fosterparents who would be willing to mail them air-tickets?

In the end, however, to Joseph's great relief, she agreed. She would write personally to the American couple making it clear Joseph was not to be spoiled. And that he was to be back within a month, before he could become entirely corrupted by American ways, to resume his place among those as unfortunate as he was. Unless they wanted to keep him in America for good, which they showed no intention of doing.

The next few weeks passed in a frenzy of preparation. The ticket had to arrive, a flight had to be booked, a passport had to be issued to Joseph, a visa obtained. He was given a little suitcase for his clothes, and he swelled with pride at his tangible evidence of possessions. He had things, he was somebody. With a passport, a suitcase, a ticket, he was not just a little brown face in a crowd around the gruel bowl; he was Master Joseph Kumaran, and he was going somewhere.

And finally, wearing the tight blazer he had been given on the morning of his departure, its pocket stuffed with the news-magazine clipping he had hoarded since it had been shown to him by Sister Celine four years ago, his passport nestling next to a glossy colour photo of his hosts sent to him so that he would recognize them at the airport, Joseph was put on board the plane. Sister Celine was there to see him off, she smiled at him through misty glasses, and Joseph felt the wetness on her cheeks when she hugged him at the departure gate. But he could not cry in return; he was a little scared, but more excited than upset, and he certainly was not sad.

The man sitting next to him did not seem to care particularly for the movie after all. Twice, Joseph caught him dozing off, his eyes closing and his chin sinking slowly to his chest; twice, with equal suddenness, his neighbour's head would jerk awake, prompted no doubt by some startling sound on the earphones. The third time this happened, the man pulled off his earphones in disgust and strode off, clambering over Joseph, in quest of a wash-basin.

Joseph could not resist this opportunity. It was too good to be true: earphones plugged in, next to him, unused. He eased himself out of his seatbelt and sat in his neighbour's chair. Then,

22

tentatively, looking around him to make sure no one had noticed him, he raised the tips to his ears. Almost immediately he was assaulted by the sounds of the movie: brakes screeched as a car drew to a halt; a man dashed down some stairs with a gun in his hand; there was some panting dialogue; the gun went off, the bullet's report a deafening symphony in Joseph's ear; a woman screamed. And his neighbour returned from the toilet.

Joseph looked up, almost in agony. His pleasure had been so brief.

The man smiled down at him from the aisle. 'Mine, sonny,' he beamed.

Joseph had been well brought up. 'Excuse me,' he said, gently removing the earphones and placing them on the seat. He slid into his place again, his neighbour returned to his chair, the earplugs went back on, and Joseph found he could not see the screen through his tears.

Hoping his neighbour would not notice, he dabbed at his eyes with the clean, white handkerchief Sister Angela had pressed into his hand that morning. That morning—it seemed so long ago. He returned the handkerchief to his pocket, feeling once again the magazine clipping that, four years ago, had started him on this journey. Resolutely, he refrained from pulling it out. That was not him: he had another identity now. He took out his passport, and his eyes caressed each detail on the inside page, from the fictional birthdate ('It's easier than going through the entire "birthdate unknown" business,' Sister Eva had declared) to the inventory of his characteristics ('Hair: black; eyes: black; skin: brown') to the new, awkward photograph. Joseph staring glassy-eyed into the studio camera. And then, returning the passport at long last to his inside pocket, he touched the other photo, the glossy, colour portrait of his new, albeit temporary, parents. After some hesitation, he took it out: these were the people whose house he would call home for the next month.

But would he really? He stared at their forms in the photograph. They had sent Joseph their picture so he would recognize them, but they had not asked for his. 'We're sure we'll spot him as soon as he gets off the plane,' the wife had written to Sister Celine. 'We feel we've known him all our lives.' Joseph had felt flattered then, deeply touched. Then one day, in a fit of temper, Sister Eva had threatened to replace Joseph with another little dark-skinned boy from the orphanage. 'Do you think they'd be able to tell the difference?' she had demanded.

In silent, desperate misery, Joseph had not known what to say.

Looking at the photograph, Joseph tried to think of the magic of America, of things there he had heard about and dreamed of—movies, parties, delicious food of infinite variety, outings to the beach and to Disneyland. But his eyes dilated and the photograph blurred. He did not know why he felt suffused with a loneliness more intense, more bewildering in its sadness than he had ever experienced in the gruel crowds of HELP. He was alone, lost somewhere between a crumpled magazine clipping and the glossy brightness of a colour photograph.

On the seat next to him, his neighbour snored peacefully, chin resting in surrender on his chest, earphones imbedded into the sides of his head. On the screen, the magic images flickered, cascaded and danced on.

Wanted: A Broom

when he said Darling
he didn't ask for a paisa for anything
but when he said Marry Me
he asked for gold
money
stuff
plates and pots
everything
aiyo he even asked for a broom
to sweep the floor
I said
the broom's the limit
he got up and asked why

I said
so I can sweep you from my heart
and toss you in the trash

paying a life-subscription
just to get a male hooker
what am I
half-crazy
or a total fool

Translated from the Tamil by Martha Ann Selby
and K. Paramasivam

If Hot Flowers Come to the Street

Red cassia flowers
are a forest fire,
or so they say.
It's an April event
called a summer flower.
Anarchy in green.
An explosion of buds.
Fire in the snow.

On the head of Lord Siva
of the snow mountains
there are red matted locks,
        gleaming cassia blossoms,
        and the Ganges.

In his red hand,
        fire,
        a small drum,
        a deer.

And a snake at his throat.
That snake
won't strike the deer.
The fire in his hand
won't burn the Ganges.

But in our street,
even flies will swarm
to hot flowers.

Translated from the Tamil by Martha Ann Selby
and K. Paramasivam

Dream Face*

That night, I saw the Holy Prophet in a dream. He was standing at the edge of a field, talking to some farmers, and rays of light were streaming through the waving ears of wheat.

His appearance was as I remembered it from hearing about it every day. He wore a large white turban on his head, and had a green robe wrapped around his body.

When the farmers finished speaking, a smile flashed upon his face. The farmers placed their hands across their stomachs—he raised his right hand and explained something to them. They nodded their heads as in agreement. Then he bid good-bye to them and slowly walked away along the raised edge of the field. His green robe became part of the field's greenery, and he was absorbed into the world's expanse.

I was very young then.

In the morning, I told my mother about my dream. She clapped both hands on her ears in astonishment and said, 'Wahe Guru! Good fortune is on its way.'

She ran to the stairs that went to our roof. When she reached the fourth step, she glanced over the wall and called out, 'Sister Fatima!'

After a little while, the face of a woman as old as my mother appeared. She wore large dangling ear-rings in her ears, and a black wrap about her head.

'What is it, Ram Pyari?' she asked simply, as if such a call were an everyday occurrence.

---

* The translators wish to thank Seemi Ghazi for her help during the process of translation.

My mother replied in a conspiratorial tone, 'Did you hear what ɔur Chhandi dreamt last night?'

'No. What was it?'

My mother related the dream I had seen to sister Fatima.

'Allah, no!' exclaimed Fatima with complete reverence, Where is he now?'

My mother said, 'He's playing with some kids down there in ;he lane.'

Fatima said, 'God, what a reward in heaven the little wretch has earned!' and her face disappeared off the wall.

I was playing hopscotch with the other children in the lane. It was afternoon, and there was silence all around. At such a time, the bellowing of the cows and buffaloes tied to various doors sounded strange. Maybe they were itching to go for a swim in the canal. But the herdsman had not yet come. The girls' school had not yet completed its day.

Hopscotch is a strange game. One makes wells, rivers, and seas by drawing lines on the ground. The toss of an empty tin of shoe polish decides which part of the universe one will leap across today. It was my turn, and I was poised to fly across the third river when Fatima grabbed me from behind in a bear-hug.

'Allah, what's happened? Tell me all about it. God, you're all flushed, what distinction you've gained!'

Picking me up, she carried me towards her house. Mother was watching the scene from above. All the kids stood holding their breath, worried about their play—now that one player had suddenly been lifted from the game, how would they organize everything again?

Fatima's husband, Shaikh Allah Ditta, sold cane and bamboo in the market below the house. The long poles were useful in erecting tents and pavilions; people also used them to build houses. The short sticks were good for lances and spears, which were later used to beat and to kill. Fatima had sent word to him. He came, bearing a white cotton for pajamas for me, poplin for a shirt, a pound of *jalebis** and one-and-a quarter rupees in cash. Fatima put everything in my lap, then fell to the ground in contemplation.

---

* Jalebis: fried sweets dipped in syrup.

Shaikh Allah Ditta knelt with his head between both knees. Fatima began to mutter in a voice moist with tears, 'Our Prophet, our very own Prophet!'

Shaikh Allah Ditta moved his head from side to side as if in ecstasy, whispering, 'Amen . . . Amen!'

The clocktower in the town square struck half past twelve. A bell rang and the girls were let out of school. The cows and buffaloes ran bellowing to the canal as soon as their ropes were loosened. One group of kids defeated another by a game. There was noise all around, a noise like the end of the world.

Many years have passed since this incident.

The tower in the town square must still strike the hours. The bell in the girls' school must still ring and dismiss the students. Cows and buffaloes must still run bellowing to the canal, and the wells, rivers, and seas drawn on the ground must still be crossed. But no sound reaches me.

'Mother, why haven't I dreamt another dream like that one?' I asked.

'Son, how can you? They remained on the other side. We had to come here,' she replied.

All of a sudden, Mother had fallen sick. We had her treated, but nothing worked. One day, the doctor said, 'It would be better if you admitted her to a sanatorium.'

After much running around, we got her a place in the sanatorium of Usgaon. Mother stayed there for three-and-a-half years. My wife and I were with her on the evening before the day of her death. She seemed absolutely fine. Her face was glowing, and her eyes had a sparkle in them. Margaret, the nurse, had combed her silver-grey hair and knotted it into a bun at the back of her head. She had never appeared healthier to us. Both of us returned by the evening bus, since the children were all alone at home. And Margaret had said in a reassuring tone, 'You can go. Mother is doing well.'

Margaret took care of the sanatorium, and had become my adoptive sister by tying a *rakhi** on my wrist. It had happened quite

---

* Rakhi: A Hindu festival which celebrates affectionate ties between brothers and sisters, real and adoptive. The sister ties a golden thread around the brother's wrist to commemorate the bond.

by coincidence: one day, I was visiting Mother and it was the festival of Rakhi. I sat by Mother's bedside, talking of this and that, when Margaret appeared and tied the gilded string around my wrist. I was surprised and confused.

'Mother has made me her daughter,' she explained.

Mother was like that. She could enchant people wherever she went. I remember that my father was madly in love with her till the day he died. Often I saw that he would stroke Mother's cheeks, then fix an intense gaze on her face and cry.

Father would say to me, 'Son, don't ever bring prejudice into your mind. Keep your faith strong, and accept what you read as sent by God. Otherwise you won't understand anything. You'll just remain a nitwit of a Qamruddin all your life.' He had a strange habit. If he didn't know someone's name, or thought him a fool, he would call him 'Qamruddin.' His words proved true at many points in my life. Every so often I have seen some Qamruddin, with his rote memory, get the job. Strapping height, long arm, and a broad smile plastered across his face—who weighs the brains in his head?

Mother's corpse had grown cold. We received the news on the afternoon of the next day. Margaret gave our address to a sanatorium servant and dispatched him to us. I reached Usgaon with my wife and the children. Margaret sat mournfully at the door of the sanatorium's morgue. As soon as we arrived she hugged all of us turn by turn and wept. We performed Mother's last rites in a small cremation ground right there in Usgaon. It was as if a chapter in life's book ended with her.

After that day, Usgaon became a place of pilgrimage for us. Every year at Rakhi, we would go there. Margaret would tie a *rakhi* on my wrist and then we would go to the cremation ground and sit and talk of Mother. It was almost as if Margaret became a member of our family since that day.

*

The bus was trundling along at its own peculiar pace towards Usgaon. Outside I saw the same scene, well-known from many other visits.

31

'You'll die a dog's death, you son of a bitch,' one Qamruddin jokingly swore at another beside him on the seat behind me. I turned to look at them, just once, then continued to watch the all too familiar sights outside the window.

Two parallel ranges of hills kept apace of each other. Their crests were covered with mist. The sky above them was patched with clouds. In their shallow laps were a few houses with roofs of red tile. One had an open window, another its door ajar. The insides of the houses were dark. Nothing inside was visible. The air was heavy, rich with the smell of moist earth. The upper branches of the trees swung in a regular rhythm. The moving bus seemed to stand still.

The next day was Rakhi and I was on my way to Usgaon, alone this time, to have Margaret tie the *rakhi* on my wrist.

Usgaon, properly speaking, is divided into three parts. The first part has a magnificent temple, the pinnacle of whose dome can be seen from far away. A saffron flag flies on it. The temple is built on a grand scale, and a high boundary wall surrounds it and its guesthouse. All the rooms in the guesthouse are air-conditioned; they are always occupied by the foreign devotees of the Swamiji in whose name the temple was built.

Who was that Swamiji? No one really knew. A pure soul, he appeared one day on this piece of earth and became one with it. One sees his picture everywhere. He wears only a loincloth, and the rest of his body is entirely naked. With one hand raised in a benedictory gesture, he sits like a god blessing the world before him. In some pictures, there is a fearsome snake coiled in front of him. Though its hood is raised it seems to have been mesmerized by his powerful gaze. The great hall of the temple is filled with mystery and darkness. In it glitters its reigning deity, a golden figure of Swamiji. Swamiji had been dark-skinned and fat; his face was round like a football. Day and night, *arti** is performed before his image at regular intervals. All the local and foreign followers participate. One devotee accompanies them on a harmonium. Several loudspeakers pick up the song and spread it in the sky above the temple. The entire scene appears as if the Creator himself had wished it to be so.

---

* Arti: ceremony of worship.

On one side of the main temple building is the office of a foreign bank. In front of the office stands a very neat and clean restaurant. A path leads from the restaurant to the park behind the temple. There are fruit trees in the park, as well as beds of many different flowers. Here, local and foreign devotees sit around scattered tables, sipping coffee and gossiping. Next to the restaurant is a post-office named after the temple. Outside the post-office is a bus-stand. Across the paved road are a few more stores; one of them is a laundry, another a provision store. Far from there, in a house beside the main road, there is a 'foreign liquor' shop. The air remains filled with the melody of the *arti*; there is always a lot of life on the street.

In the second part of Usgaon is the sanatorium.

Far removed from the city's dust and the factories' poisonous air, disease-infected old men and women shuffle around the sanatorium grounds, drawing a few dearly purchased breaths. Or else they can be found sprawled on deck-chairs in the sun, peering at the sky through their hands. There are sulphur springs in this area. Swimsuit-clad foreign devotees as well as local men and women, with towels thrown across their shoulders, can often be seen as they come and go. If there is constant activity to purify the soul in the temple section of Usgaon, then in this section there is an equally constant effort to make or to keep the body free of disease. Both parts are full of life. People spend money and lead spiritual or physical lives. Margaret's house is in this part of town, behind the sanatorium.

When we visit Usgaon, we always stay at Margaret's house; she stays with us when she comes to the city. Didn't I tell you that we are now almost members of one family?

The third part of Usgaon is a tiny village.

This village must have been settled centuries ago. Many a storm must have blown away its thatched roofs, then hundreds of dark hands must have put up new homes. The fields spread around the homes are eons old. The people living in this part of Usgaon must have gathered the crop destined for them from these fields millions of times. Those who live in these homes are always half-naked. Their bodies have turned jet black in the heat of the sun. The breasts of their women hang like ripe fruit from trees.

Their ears are pierced with many holes, each filled with a dangling silver ring. Their homes are dark; their women must walk to two distant, filthy ponds to fetch jars of water.

The village is centuries away from the temple section of Usgaon, but a paved road travels from there to here and then disappears in a field. Endless tracks begin here. They go past the houses, cut across the fields, and break away to endless places.

Once when I came here wandering aimlessly, I suddenly found myself at the field where I had seen rays of light streaming through the waving ears of wheat, the field where I had seen a group of farmers talking to 'him.' 'So that's the wheat field of my childhood,' I had said to myself and stood there for a long time waiting. The sun was hot and there was a stillness all around. Only the wind could be heard whistling overhead, less often the chirping of a bird. But no one came here. The green crop in the field kept waving in the breeze.

I got down at the bus stop and, picking up my bag, marched off towards Margaret's house. These roads were familiar; I could walk to her house blindfolded. At one place on the way I noticed a crowd. A few cars and some police vehicles also stood there. Several men, dressed in shining bright white clothes, were busy making some sort of arrangement. A small canopy had been set up in an open space, its coloured canvas fluttering in the wind. The inside of the canopy was decorated with paper bunting. On one side were a large table and several chairs. I walked over to take a look. When I came close I saw that there was a handpump set up under the canopy; thick flower garlands had been placed around it. Nearby a small fire was lit for the *havan**, and a brahmin, naked from the waist up, was conducting the sacred ritual. I was informed that the regional minister had come to inaugurate the handpump, to make it easy for the villagers to obtain drinking water.

Incense was burning in the *havan* fire and the air was filled with the sound of mantras. As the chanting would reach a climax, several people poured more incense and oil into the fire, including the minister who wore a thick garland identical to those around the handpump.

---

* Havan: a sacrificial ritual.

When the ritual ended, the minister smashed a coconut on the handpump. Everybody clapped loudly and shouted, 'Long live the minister sahib!' The minister moved the handle of the pump up and down and water poured out of the pump's mouth. That first water was quickly caught in a pot and distributed among the people present, like holy water at a temple. Everyone received it in their cupped palms, raised it to their lips to drink, then reverently wiped their wet fingers dry on their hair.

When I explained to Margaret why it took me so long to reach her house, she said, 'Yes, those poor villagers have a big water problem. They have to drink water from filthy ponds. It's good that something has been done.'

We decided that she should tie the *rakhi* in the morning, then I'd catch the first bus back to the city, leaving at 8:30. Then Margaret went off to the sanatorium to make her final round for the day. I lay down on her bed to rest, but very soon I fell asleep.

Margaret woke me when she came back. It was late and she had already set the table. We ate, and then she urged me to sleep there on her bed, while she herself went to sleep in the other room. The food and weariness from the long bus journey had me fast asleep in no time.

Then a strange dream effect began. The dream that I had as a child, Fatima's glowing face, Mother's burning corpse, so many other familiar and unfamiliar faces began to circle round as if hanging on long threads from the ceiling. I wanted so much to see 'him' again the way he had appeared in my childhood dream. That vision was as if held hostage somewhere. Then the clutches of my senses loosened and I was off into another world.

My nostrils filled with the smell of a body. Suddenly I tore apart the web of sleep and sat up with a jerk.

'What have I done?' I muttered angrily. The answer was, nothing. I had merely seen something happening. But whatever I had seen or done, it had been a shameful act. I was disgusted with myself. Despite the long journey from the jungle of ignorance to the valley of civilization, my mind was not enlightened. The room was pitch dark. I lit a match, it was half past three.

That shameful act had numbed all my senses. My mind couldn't think at all. It felt as if someone were hammering in my ears. I turned on the light, lit a cigarette, and started pacing the room.

'God, how did this happen?' I whispered to myself. I could not calm down. I'd had sex with Margaret in my dream.

In the morning I got ready very early. Margaret came into the room. She tied a *rakhi* on my wrist and put a sweet in my mouth. I gave her one hundred and one rupees. We were both silent. Everything happened mechanically. Then I picked up my bag.

'So soon?' asked Margaret.

'I'll walk slowly. You'll have to leave soon too, for your duties,' I replied in a sinking voice, and quickly walked out.

On my way I again found myself near that field where rays of light had streamed through the ears of wheat in my dream. I stopped there for some time, hoping I would be purified. But no one appeared. 'Who am I waiting for?' I asked myself. There was no answer this time. The sun rose slowly from behind the hill. There was no one next to the wheat field.

I started walking towards the main road. Soon I reached the spot where the canopy had been set up yesterday. It was gone. The sacred fire was dead. Remnants of the puja were scattered around. The garlands around the pump had wilted. Then I saw a half-naked, dark-skinned woman coming from the village; she had a clay pot on her head. As she walked straight towards the pump I noticed the silver rings in her ears and the tattoo on her forehead; her hair was loose on top but drawn into a bun at the back.

I thought: she's the first woman to carry home water to drink from the handpump. I stayed to watch that first gush of water.

The woman came to the pump and put the pot down on the ground. Then, with folded hands and bowed head, she saluted the handpump. Straightening up, she put the pot back on her head and walked away, towards the filthy pond where she had always gone to get water to drink.

Translated from the Urdu by Aditya Behl and C. M. Naim

Questions

A question has no answer
it has four sides
four or more directions—
one mine, one that came before me,
one that will come after me . . . and the fourth?
The fourth is the question's own, the one all around me,
    mine and yours and everyone's together.

That's the only true direction
the true one--
it makes us understand,
it cajoles us, shakes us awake, embraces us,
scatters everything inside and outside,
pacifies us, holds us still.

And yet we remain beyond it
each one alone, as we were before
like the question itself at the beginning—
helpless, like an unambiguous 'Yes, yes' for an answer,
we don't even see each other
in the mist of forgetfulness that comes down
    from the empty spaces beyond us.

We want the question to be
like the first ray of the sun
red, round, slicing through things vertically
because later we'll never be again
as enormous as that deceptive, troublesome question
        without direction.

Translated from the Marathi by Vinay Dharwadker

Snapshot

the seventeen lions woven into
the carpet are set free
in the vacant body of the woman
hanging by a rope

the glass goat in the corner
takes an unearthly leap
and goes over the edges
of the woman hanging by a rope

the empty vase flashes
like a flashbulb and prints
on the heavenly negatives
of the snapshot of a suicide

those dazzling blinding flowers
which burn the viewer's eyes

Translated from the Marathi by Vinay Dharwadker

Language of Communication

Something—
which the mailman never brings
something—
which falls all day
like dust from the rooftops

Something—
which we're in a hurry to catch
because of which
    we miss the bus
    we let the cup of tea stand
    untouched on the table
    we aren't shocked or hurt
    by the news of killing in the city
all that happens
is that a man gets up
picks up his comb
and sets it down even closer to the mirror

Something—
for which all the pencils weep in their sleep
and the houses at the two ends of a street
stand there for years
without a word
in one straight line

Translated from the Hindi by Vinay Dharwadker

Blank Page

On a blank page
there's no dawn no dusk
there's a midnight sun
shining down on it
from beyond the hemisphere

Look closely
you can see a pair of pale eyes
glittering there
the fire of a tiger's lovely coat
is leaping and spreading on your desk

Reach out and run your fingers
through this violent fur
there's nothing to fear
a blank page
is soft and gentle like your skin
ancient like your love
free like your hatred
civilized like your fingernails
and salty like your blood

Touch it
it feels like the pulse
in your neck

This is what poetry does
this simple and terrible thing—
after all our words
it always leaves us
with a blank page

Translated from the Hindi by Vinay Dharwadker

The Book of Benoy

It all began with something I overheard one day. I was sitting at the A-1 restaurant, drinking my tea and eating a tomato omelette when I looked across at the table next to mine.

You know what the tables are like, marble-topped and with plump jars of tomato sauce. Well, there was this man at the table, a big, broad-shouldered man and he was pouring the sauce lavishly onto a mutton cutlet. Drowning the thing in sauce. You've heard the phrase: drowning one's sorrows? Well, this man was drowning his in tomato sauce.

I know what you're thinking: that I'm crazy, fanciful, have a wasp in my ear, and that sort of thing. But it isn't so.

The man's heart was broken and I knew it. Why this was so, of course I couldn't tell. But the man was broken-hearted and I knew it.

It was at this time that the waiter came up to his table and I waited with bated breath. (I'm a bachelor and I live in a boarding house—if you've done that yourself, well, then you'll know how it is. One learns to eavesdrop—make no mistake, there's no *malice* intended. Well, all right, perhaps on occasion, but what's a conversation after all but a slice of life? Well, that's how I see it.)

Anyhow, to get back to my story, the man had taken a dog-eared notebook out of his pocket and he was kissing it. Kissing it with the reverence one would show a holy relic.

'Books save lives,' he said to the waiter. 'Yesterday I might have hanged myself but for this.' And then his face lit up with a smile that had the radiance of a thousand suns.

Quite blinding, and for an instant we blinked. All of us

consuming our omelettes, our cutlets and our brain masalas at the A-1 restaurant. We blinked.

So, where does that leave us? With a flash of insight! In that moment, you see, I knew.

I'm a soldier of a sort. One of the great army of the unemployed that haunts this city—patrols it almost, you might say. Only, I belong to the officer cadre, as it were. I'm squeamish.

A fatal failing as it were and it was why for the last six months I had been jobless. I worked for the Ministry of Eternal Affairs and I'd refused a bribe. It isn't all that uncommon—there are numbers enough of my ilk, but I was unfortunate. My superiors got to hear. And within a month I was out on my ear.

'Can't have his kind around!' I'd heard one of them roar and I'd quivered.

I had no defense. 'You're a fool, Benoy,' a colleague had scolded. 'If you must refuse a bribe, be discreet about it. There's an art in not conforming. There's a skill to these things.'

Alas, too true. I am no artist.

So, there I was huddled in my room, my nervous tic getting the better of me, endlessly circling in red Job Openings.

I survived on *upma** brought to my room by my kindly landlady, a Mrs Rawal. A generous soul with the heart of a philanthropist. 'Can't have you starving, Mr Roy,' she insisted. And charged me only the cost price for my meals.

I have a theory about this city. It endures on the goodness of neighbours.

Anyhow, there I was, in a state of suspension and eating my omelette at the A-1 restaurant, when a chance remark by a stranger changed the course of my life.

'Pearl Harbor'—that was the name of the second-hand bookshop in whose direction I headed the next morning. It was one of those mornings that has an air of being spruced up about it.

I liked that. I like things to be ironed and in their place. It's almost a fetish with me, you might say. It was why I'd kept an iron in my desk at the Ministry—the red tape on *my* files had always been ironed.

---

* Upma: a breakfast dish made out of semolina.

Quirky, perhaps, but that's how I am. A man can't change his nature overnight, now, can he?

I turned a corner and there it was. The green shutters of the windows had been thrown open and a peon with a broom was sweeping the leaves of a book into a gutter.

I hurried forward. 'What on earth are you doing?' I demanded in indignation. 'That's no way to treat a book.'

For a moment the man looked startled. It's an effect I sometimes have on people. My eyebrows, like bushy wings, disappear into my hairline—a source of some embarrassment to me, but Mrs Rawal once assured me that it made me seem 'learned.'

The man recovered his composure swiftly enough and glared at me. I trembled. 'Who are you?' he said rudely. 'The Boss? When the Boss says sweep a book into the gutter, I do it. That's what I'm paid to do and I do it.'

What could I say? The man's logic was irrefutable.

I cleared my throat. 'Your Boss?' I said. 'Is he in town?'

'He's always in town,' was the answer and gingerly I stepped into the shop.

I'd been inside the shop before, of course. On several occasions, drawn to it by the name on the signboard. 'Pearl Harbor.' There was a suggestion of Poetry about the name and although I'd never actually encountered the Boss I'd been curious about him.

'Hello,' I said, 'is anyone here? I've come about the notice in the papers. Assistant required?'

It was as if a mist cleared. If you've ever spent the night beside a swamp, you'll know what I mean. You wake in the morning to the moist sound of insects and like a drifting dream the mist begins to clear.

Suddenly it seemed like a very different place from the shop I'd visited earlier. It was still untidy but now I could read the titles of the books. Growing in the centre beneath a tube-light was a vine with lilac flowers. Tiny blooms with a velvety sheen and a purple stripe down the centre.

Above it, a wasps' nest.

'You're not a botanist, are you?' asked a voice and I whirled around. It was the most mellifluous voice I'd ever heard and it

45

belonged to a small woman not more than 4′7″ in height. (Serafina, the Boss's sister, I later learned.)

'The job's yours,' the woman said.

And that's how I got it.

I'd been working at the bookshop for a week, when one day the strangest thing happened.

*

I'd just cleared a shelf of its books and was about to dust it when a high voice called out. 'You, over there. You work here?'

'I do,' I said. 'Can I help you?'

The woman was a small creature with black curls and a red hibiscus in her hair. 'Yes,' she said, 'you can.' She was an imperious little thing with flashing eyes and red lips.

I swallowed hard.

'I want a book,' she said. 'Do you have it? *Images of Thunder?* I believe it went out of print a few years ago.'

'I'm sure I can find you a copy, ma'am,' I said and scurried off. I've been told there's something of the beetle about me—a rapid scurry and the twitching of antennae, I suppose! I comfort myself that these are useful virtues in an Assistant of any kind.

Anyhow, I found what the woman wanted but before I could write out a bill she'd snatched it from my hand and flung it into the centre of the room. 'Denounced,' she cried.

And before I could so much as gather my wits about me, she had me rushing around the bookshop in search of book after book. 'Denounced,' she'd cry each time, throwing the book into the centre of the room.

I'd seen strange things in my time at the Ministry but never anything quite like this.

The sweat streamed down my back and, what with all the rushing around and the 'denounceds' ringing in my ears, I was in quite a state, I can tell you. As any self-respecting Assistant might be.

'Ma'am,' I protested feebly as the pile in the centre of the room grew to monstrous proportions, but the Hibiscus Lady was in no mood to listen.

'Hurry,' she said, 'time's running out. Denounced!' Her voice had grown quite hoarse by this time, what with all the denouncing she was doing, but she was what you'd call the 'stick-with-it' type. She had a mission to accomplish and she was going to do it!

I'd begun to wilt. Nothing in the Ministry had prepared me for this—I could feel my nervous tic beginning to come on and might have collapsed onto the floor if at that moment Serafina (the Boss's sister, if you remember) had not burst into the room.

'What on earth?' she cried, stopping short. 'Who's responsible for this?'

She swivelled round and glared at the Hibiscus Lady. Now there's something about Serafina that's irresistible—a sort of blazing charm at its best, and a searing rage at its worst. In that short week I'd grown to love her—madly, silently, and with a beetle's devotion.

'Benoy,' she demanded, 'have you gone mad? What are you up to? Books, you know, are not for kindling.'

The Hibiscus Lady smiled. 'Aren't they?'

And that was a mistake. You see there's something of the firecracker about Serafina—light her fuse and she's in no mood for debate.

The Hibiscus Lady smiled, Serafina glared, and before my very eyes I saw the smile freeze on the Hibiscus Lady's face and her flesh turn to stone. (I've seen the public petrified at the Ministry, slowly turn over the years into fossils—it's the waiting that does it—but *never* anything like this!)

One moment the woman was flesh and blood and then within minutes she was granite.

'Serafina,' I whispered, quite stunned I can tell you, 'what have you done?'

'Trade secret,' she said, dusting her hands. 'If you want to run a bookshop, these days, it's a skill you acquire. Or it's the cinders for you.'

'What do we do with her?' I said.

'Stack her at the back,' said Serafina. 'She'll come in useful one day. You'll see.'

*

And she was right. 'Books save lives,' the stranger had said at the A-1 restaurant and on 15 June I was to discover just how they did it.

It was one of those monsoon days with the rain pelting down in angry sheets, but undaunted and with all my antennae quivering, I hurried to work with the rest of the city—dodging the traffic here, a cow there—until I reached the bookshop, panting and a little breathless, but not entirely bedraggled, given the day.

Serafina was already in and she greeted me with a cheery, 'Good morning, Benoy. Bright day, isn't it?'

I gave her a watery smile. Much as I love her, I can't say I think much of her wit.

Anyhow, we buckled down to work over a pile of books to be priced when all of a sudden the door squeaked open.

'The rain's stopped,' Serafina said, glancing outside. 'Why don't we send Keshav (the peon) for some tea?'

But I wasn't listening. Four men had entered the shop and I recognized one of them at once. The Weasel. My blood ran cold.

'Still in business?' the Weasel said strolling up to Serafina.

'Yes,' she said, 'and I intend to stay that way. What can we do for you?'

'Don't waste my time,' the Weasel said. 'I sent round a circular last week to all the bookshops in this city—only such-and-so books to be sold. No more.'

'There's been no circular,' I protested. (Anyone who's worked in a Ministry recognizes a circular—that's what they're there for.)

'Oh, yes, there has, Benoy,' snapped Serafina. 'I didn't show it to you.'

'Well,' said the Weasel looking around, 'I see you've done nothing about it. Most of these books are proscribed.'

'On whose authority?'

'Mine.'

'I don't recognize it.'

'Don't recognize the Authority of the Mob?' The Weasel gave a great hoot of laughter and the men who were with him gurgled like babies.

What, I thought, was Serafina going to do this time? It was all right to turn the Hibiscus Lady into a gargoyle but a whole mob? There'd be nowhere to store them.

What I'd forgotten, but Serafina Gomes hadn't, was that Books, you see, have a Life in them. They don't take kindly to being proscribed. And ours were no different.

It was at this time that we heard in the distance the sound of a howling. A chill ran up my spine. It was a howling we'd all grown to recognize in this city—the howling of the mob.

I knew what would follow—the rapid sound of shutters being pulled down. Swifter than any rattle you've ever heard, the occasional shriek. The crash and splinter of glass—rocks heaved through a window. And a family's trade gone up in smoke. The spit and crackle of orange flames.

In this city you learned an early lesson. You learned all about the Authority of the Mob.

(Ministries are usually immune to this danger, but then ministries are usually immune to most things.)

Anyhow, there we were, Serafina and I—trapped with the Weasel and his cohorts inside the shop and the mob outside.

'Ms Gomes,' I whispered, 'do as you're told, or they'll roast us alive.'

'No,' said Serafina, 'I never do as I'm told. It's a congenital defect. Prepare to burn, Benoy.'

I now resigned myself to my Fate, as it were. I was with Serafina. I loved her. I prepared to Die.

The mob was howling outside and I could feel my nervous tic stirring into action.

The Weasel, as you know, suffers from rhinitis. A congenital defect. His. It was to prove his undoing. The Weasel, you see, sneezed. (I hadn't dusted the shop in days—and what with Serafina's stubbornness, the howling of the mob outside, the tension in the air, etc. etc.—the dust had risen.)

The Weasel sneezed. And like Humpty Dumpty and the Walls of Jericho, the Books came tumbling down.

Oh, what a fall there was. A *Sarvapriya* Sanskrit to English Dictionary hit the Weasel on the head and he collapsed. Just like that. K. O'd. His cohorts collapsed too, except for one chap who managed in all that commotion to crawl to the door and throw it open.

'Get them,' he gasped. 'Get the rascals. Hang and quarter them.'

The mob howled. Once again my blood froze—and then I heard it. The stirring of a hornets' nest. Well, this was a wasp hive, but the sound's the same. (You remember, of course, that a vine with lilac flowers grew in our bookshop? And from the ceiling above it hung a wasps' nest?)

Well, like the books, the wasps had had enough.

For years they had seen the shop as hospitable terrain—and they were in no mood to suffer marauders gladly.

The wasps descended and all hell broke loose! The mob fled—and the wasps pursued them. Little black and yellow creatures buzzing in fury. Chasing that gaggle of puny men down the maze of alleyways that spread out from the shop—many-fingered, like a palm that had curled into a stinging fist.

And then we heard it—a great cry of relief. Like that hosanna which rings out when the rains first fall on the city.

(You're probably curious about the Weasel and his cohorts, aren't you? No, we didn't hang and quarter them. We sent them home in a taxi.)

'They'll be back, Serafina,' I said.

She didn't seem to mind that I'd called her that. 'I don't think so, Benoy,' she said. 'Now's when we put the Hibiscus Lady to use. We'll just mount her head above the door. Get hit by a tome, stung by a wasp or turned into stone. *That* should be warning enough. For a while anyway.' She smiled.

Oh, in that moment I'd have killed for her. My shining Serafina.

Instead, with all the calligraphic skill I'd acquired at the Ministry, I painted her a new signboard. She'd decided to rename the shop: Sarvapriya Port.

'Seems more fitting,' she said, 'given the times.'

*

I spent the next month in a state of near-bliss, I tell you. I worked as I'd never worked in any Ministry before. I didn't dare declare myself to Serafina. What beetle ever had the courage to do that? But I got that bookshop into order.

And I did it all gladly, until one day, Nemesis struck in the form of Keshav, the peon.

Keshav was devoted to Serafina and I think he'd begun to sense the cause of my preoccupations.

I tried to hide this as best I could but Passion is a strange thing, it won't be still. And so my antennae quivered with agitation when I heard her voice, my beetle carapace shone brightly in the gloom, my step became more sprightly. And none of this escaped Keshav's notice.

'Thrown out of the Ministry, weren't you?' he said one fateful afternoon.

I squirmed. 'Perhaps. How did you know?'

'I have my sources,' he said. 'They keep me informed. You're not good enough for her.'

'I don't know what you're talking about,' I said. And then with all the boldness of a creature stung to its very innards I declared, 'I have work to do even if you don't.'

'Not for long,' he said.

'What do you mean?'

'The Boss,' he said. 'Next week the Boss returns. And Serafina, she'll be leaving to get married in the District.'

I felt as though a red, hot poker had pierced me through my heart, my bowels, the very centre of my being. I howled. Mobs howl, but so too does a broken-hearted beetle. Like a madman I howled and I saw the fear flash into Keshav's eyes.

'You monster,' I cried. 'How long have you known?'

'Just this morning,' he blubbered. 'I heard just this morning . . .'

'It isn't true,' I sobbed.

'Perhaps it isn't,' he said. 'Perhaps it isn't.'

Only of course, I knew it was and I rushed out of the shop, waves of sorrow engulfing me as sauce does a mutton cutlet.

I roamed around the streets that day like an enraged creature—snarling, spitting, hissing, crackling like a short-circuited wire. And then the anger faded, and I sat on the sea wall at Sunset Drive watching the rhythm of the waves with that resignation which, all my life, had come so easily to me.

'Benoy Behari Roy,' I said to myself, 'what will you do now?'

What could I do? I returned to work. I stayed away from Serafina. I began to read.

Weeks passed. (The Boss did not return as Keshav had threatened—but I no longer cared.) I had begun another journey—a zigzag one. Physics one day. Archaeology the next. A botanist's unravelling of a plant's thirst for the sun. The elegance of a mathematical proof. And when Serafina smiled at me: the Poet.

On those nights I read the lines of the Poet—on betrayal and love and all of life's wounding. And it seemed to me as though the street lights of the city wept with me.

I'd crawl back to my beetle hole, my insect's refuge, and I'd rock myself to sleep.

I was in this state of mind when I found it. The Passion Flower. I'd taken a book down from the topmost shelf—some customer had asked for it, when the book fell open in my hands. (It was, if you recall, a second-hand bookshop and some of our books were very old indeed.)

There it lay—the petals perfectly pressed, its crimson unfaded. Miriam Rizvi, 1876. That was the name in sloping letters on the flyleaf.

'Well,' called the customer querulously, 'do you have the book or not?'

For the first time in my life, I lied. 'No,' I called back. 'We don't.'

Miriam Rizvi, 1876. Who had she been, I wondered. Miriam Rizvi. When had she slipped the flower into the book? Why? Had she been sad as I was? Bewildered and a little miserable?

So that years from then some stranger might discover the Passion Flower and in its crimson core find comfort.

Miriam Rizvi. That day she became my absent friend. I was no longer lonely any more—I spoke to her of all I read. I danced with her in my room to the music of the radio. I told her of Serafina and my sorrow—and at night before I slept I kissed the cover of the book between whose pages lay my Scarlet Heart.

I never paid for the book. I stole it. The only thing I ever stole from Serafina.

*

Serafina found out, of course. And one day as I was making out an inventory she came up behind me and said, 'Miriam Rizvi was my grandmother, you know.'

'Was she?' I cried. 'How could that be?'

'My mother's name was Bela Rizvi. She slipped that flower into the book for me when I was a child. She said that any man who saw its beauty would be the man for me. "Such a man will love books, Serafina. And the red heart of things. Trust him."

'My mother was a fanciful creature and I laughed. But she was right. Benoy,' said Serafina, 'will you marry me?'

'What about the Boss?' I found myself saying feebly. 'Isn't he coming back?'

'No,' said Serafina. 'He's going into the ammonia business.'

'And the District?' I whispered.

Serafina glared at Keshav. 'You've been listening to him, haven't you, Benoy?'

'Yes,' I said, 'I have.'

'Well, don't.'

And to think it all began with a chance remark I overheard at the A-1 restaurant.

'Books save lives,' the stranger had said. I'm not sure the Hibiscus Lady and the Weasel would agree, but then they probably have no taste for omelettes. Cauliflower ears. Or the crimson-heart of a Passion Flower.

Kannagi*

There was no end to her rage.
By its very roots she wrenched off
her breast, and hurled it

at the far domes and towers
of thousand-pillared Madurai.
Even the river was not spared—

that banner of the Pandiyan,
who, choked by her golden anklet,
slumped in his throne

never to speak again.
Did she know,
before the ladder of fire

raised her to heaven,
what would become
of her sweet Tamil country?

---

* Kannagi is the heroine of the Tamil epic, *Shilappadikaram* by Ilango Adigal (AD fifth century).

The Attar of Tamil

Your country is not a suitcase:
you are not a traveller
shuffling, with tongue in cheek,

the loose change of words.
For twenty years you have tried
to pry this book open.

Tall and attentive, the rose-apple tree*
stands in your uncle's backyard
in Trichinopoly, undefiled

by the passing English dog.
You arrive there, unscathed and with a whole skin,
with the attar of Tamil for a map.

---

* In mythology, India is a part of the Island of the Rose-Apple tree, which is one of
  the seven islands that comprise the world.

Gieve Patel

You Too

Don't think I'm new to this dumbo game!
I've seen it in and out.
So if you give me glancing,
Searing looks, and then look away
For weeks, if you let drop
A loaded word, and carry on
Thenceforth as though you never had
Said it, if you hint to me
That you are jealous of my
Other affections, then cling yourself
To your own friends in full view
Of my jealous eyes, remember,
I will remain unmoved.
Who better than you to know
I've been lashed before on this trip
All too often to care.
Hints, looks, gestures,
Fleeting, teasing offers of friendship,
Then cool withdrawal,
O drown it all in your oceans!
My smarting tears leave no
Mighty seas behind. Maybe
It's true what they say about you—
Who knows if infatuations galore don't
Torment you too, and
You weep, in hunger for the world.

The Most Beautiful Picture in the World

Kushi is playing with her younger brothers and sisters in the flooded yard of their shack when her father Subal gets home late in the afternoon from selling fish at the bazaar. Even with her back to him Kushi can tell he's had a bad day by the tone of his voice as he keeps up a flow of curses at his nine kids and his useless wife. *Bastards. Always fighting. And eat, eat, eat. Never satisfied. Eat me out of house and home. I'll show the lot of you.*

Dropping his basket on the steps, Subal yells so loudly that the pair of vultures on the nearby *taal* tree flap their wings, disturbed.

'Kushi! Get over here!'

Kushi straightens her wet sari, pulling it across her breasts and hunching her shoulders to hide the new, embarrassing curves of her body. Then reluctantly, knowing there's no way around it, she comes over to her father, who grabs a handful of her hair and booms, 'What the hell d'you think you're doing?'

Kushi struggles, tries to pull away. Subal smells of fish scales and blood, an old, dead smell. 'The flood waters brought in a *magoor* fish. We were catching it, there by the tulsi tree.'

Subal hits her hard, on the face. 'Bitch! Whore! Don't you ever think of anything but food? I should stuff that *magoor* down your throat, live. Always teaching the kids to get into trouble, instead of minding them like you're supposed to. Don't you remember your brother Nobu's just recovering from the fever? Who's going to pay for the medicine if he falls sick again?'

At the sound of Subal's shouts, Kushi's mother emerges from the dark hole of the kitchen and joins in, her fists making hollow exploding sounds on Kushi's back. 'Shit-eater! Where are the spices

I asked you to grind? Don't you ever listen to anything I say? Why don't you die and give me some peace!'

Kushi doesn't cry in spite of the beatings. She has grown used to them over her fourteen years. She knows that since the other kids are smaller and too sickly to beat, she's the one her parents most often take their anger out on. She stiffens her neck, like a calf about to ram something, then goes off to the kitchen with sulky eyes.

Later, from behind the kitchen door, Kushi watches as her mother brings Subal an aluminum *thala** filled with rice. It's the rule of their household that Subal eats first. As he has told them often enough, he's got to take care of himself. As it is, he sweats from dawn to dusk and beyond everyday just to fill the bottomless pits of their stomachs. Kushi licks her lips as Subal pours lentils over the rice, then mixes in whatever else there is—spinach, or, on good days, a minute piece of fish. He eats slowly, taking a long time, enjoying every bite. Kushi knows that he knows the children are watching hungrily from beyond the dark entrance. After lunch, he will sleep till the sun is about to set. Waking, he will slap the children around a bit, or try to mend the wicker fence, or climb the roof to count the young squash on the vines.

But none of this can hold his interest long. As soon as the lanterns are lit in the neighbouring shacks and the curved lights of VIP road tremble on the lake, Subal must slip out into the night to join his fellow fish-sellers in Kesto's toddy shop. Sometimes Kushi tries to imagine it all, the smoky tin shed with a naked bulb swinging from a wire, the musty bittersweet drink, the bursts of laughter and male jokes, the loud discussions of future plans—how they'll make a million rupees in the fish business, how they'll own their own trawlers and not have to pay that bastard wholesaler such a high commission on rotten stinking merchandise.

Once he gets back home, Kushi knows, Subal will demand dinner, thick *rotis*** with jaggery, which he'll wash down with a big pitcher of water. Then he'll yell at everyone to hurry to bed so that the kerosene lamp can be put out quickly. But Kushi knows there's another reason.

---

* Thala: a round plate.
** *Roti*: unleavened bread.

There is only one room in the shack. Everybody sleeps in there—Subal's mother behind the torn jute curtain, the children lined up against the wall, and Subal at the door so that he can grab his wife as she comes in after cleaning the kitchen. He pulls her into the corner despite her hissed protests—*I'm dead tired, been on my feet all day, your mother can hear, the children are still awake, and Kushi's getting at that age when she knows what's going on*. . . . Under his weight she struggles hopelessly, her thin arms pushing him off as soon as possible, and Kushi, lying sleepless in the dark, listens until her father's snores cut off her mother's last bitter whispers—*are you a man or a he-goat, don't you ever get sick of it, how are we going to feed another mouth* . . .

*

Something quite amazing is happening this afternoon, so amazing that Kushi stands open-mouthed on the porch, forgetting to mind her sari like her mother has told her to. Two cars have come to a stop in front of Subal's shack. The black metal doors flash blindingly as they open, and four babus wearing sahib clothes—pants, stiff white shirts, shiny shoes—emerge. They are looking for Subal! The children stop their squabbling and run up to the car, longing to touch its bright chrome fender. Subal's wife peers from the smoky kitchen, and Subal's mother shouts in a voice thin with fear, 'Subal, Subal, come and see what these babus want . . .'

The men are wearing sunglasses that glitter in the heat. They point to the house. One takes out a wallet. Subal listens to them intently, nodding. Finally, he puts out his hand for the money. The men take off the sunglasses and smile, their hot eyes roaming over Kushi's ripe body, and hand him fifteen rupees.

'Subal, what is it? What do they want? Why did they give you money? Are they trying to buy the house or what?' Kushi hears her grandmother quaver from the shack entrance.

'Quit screaming in my ear, Mother. No one's trying to buy anything,' Subal yells from habit, but Kushi can see he's too pleased over the money to be irritated by anything anyone says right now. Fifteen rupees! Almost a week's income! And he had to do nothing to get it! It's like the money fell directly from heaven into his hands!

'Then what's the money for? You haven't done something you shouldn't, have you, like Nitai from down the street last month? I didn't like the way those babus were looking at the girl. You didn't . . . ?'

'Don't be stupid. Isn't that just like a woman, jumping to filthy conclusions! They're going to put up a picture here on my land—that's what the money is for. And I'll get it every month!'

'Picture? What picture?'

'An advertisement. That's . . . oh, what's the use, you won't understand. Now don't waste any more of my time. I've got to go down to Kesto's about something important.'

*

The very next day a truck carrying necessary equipment arrives. Men bustle about with noisy machines, scaring away the vultures from the *taal* tree. Two steel girders are thrust into the soil and screwed in place. Above them looms the picture, huge and intoxicatingly blue. In its upper right corner is an airplane in flight. Far to the left, a magic city, the tall buildings glittering like temple spires amid golden clouds. Below, on golden sands, a young golden-haired couple, holding hands, running. How fair-skinned they are! How brightly their teeth gleam in that heavenly light! Subal's entire family stands below the picture, admiring the sahib's strong muscles, the bright pink of his woman's lips and cheeks, her bold curves, the way her lacy dress clings to her beautiful thighs.

Kushi is especially entranced by the picture. She's never seen any human being as beautiful as the two up there. They seem like gods, so young, so full of laughter, running forever without tiring. She wishes there was someone she could tell this to. But her grandmother is busy making sure Subal will buy her a blanket before winter comes, now that he has all this money; her brother Haran, the only one who attends school, is begging for a new pen and a notebook; and mother in her nagging voice is saying something about clothes, especially a blouse for Kushi, who's growing like a weed, and have you seen how men have started staring at her, and her all exposed in her torn sari? Kushi stands there a long time, caressing the girders, looking up at the dazzling blue sheen of the picture, and when her brother Nobu, the precocious one, mother's pet, calls out, 'Hey look, you can see all the way up that woman's leg,' she gives him a resounding slap, though she knows she'll have to pay for it later.

*

At night Kushi sits outside the kitchen, kneading dough for *rotis*. She hates *rotis*. They take so long to roll out, and they're gone in a minute. Besides, she only gets two as her share, just enough to whet that constant gnawing hunger she cannot remember ever being without. Outside, night has fallen. The frogs are calling from the pond. Kushi hears rustling, flapping sounds from the *taal* tree. The vultures must have returned. Subal is still at the toddy shop, celebrating the picture. Kushi turns around to look for it, but, disappointingly, it has disappeared into the darkness. A sound like a night-bird's cry pierces the shadows. Kushi wipes her hands and looks around for the silhouette of her grandmother, nodding on the porch.

'Granny, can you do a few *roti*s for me? I'll massage your feet at night for you if you do. I'll be back in a minute.'

'Oh . . . OK, but just a few now, mind.'

'Why? Where does madam think she is going in the dark?' This from her mother, who has been noisily frying something in the kitchen. God! That woman has ears like a she-wolf!

'To the outhouse. Is that permitted?' Kushi puts into her voice the right amount of sarcasm, enough to shut her mother up, but not enough to bring on a spate of blows.

Once outside, Kushi runs past the bamboo grove which serves as their outhouse, darts across V.I.P. road with its honking cars, and pushes past the shrubs which line the lake. A strong arm grips her and a male voice close to her ear whispers, 'Look what I brought for you today, my golden girl. Potato pakoras! I know how much you love them.'

The hot oil smell of the fried potatoes that appear miraculously in front of her face floods Kushi's insides. She begins to stuff them into her mouth with both hands. The man makes use of this opportunity to pull her against him and find her young breasts. His hands are hard, the fingers cracked and calloused from working at the cycle factory, but Kushi doesn't mind. In her whole life, has anyone given her so many good things to eat, called her by so many sweet names?

'Tabu-da, don't you want some, too? The pakoras are just delicious. Hey, you're tickling me.'

'Shhh! Don't laugh so loud. Some son-of-a-bitch might hear you! Come closer.'

'Tabu-da, not there! You told me you wouldn't! Now remove your hand or I'll scream and then someone will *really* hear!'

'OK, OK, you silly girl.'

Tabu moves his hand reluctantly to Kushi's hip. His fingers caress her taut behind, waiting for another opportunity.

'Do you know Tabu-da, something wonderful happened today.'

'What?' says Tabu as he tries to manoeuver her onto the ground without being too obvious about it.

Kushi lowers her voice into a conspiratorial whisper. 'A picture! They put up a picture at our house today!'

'What picture?' Tabu has managed to get her where he wants, but Kushi doesn't notice, although the ground is damp under her back.

'It's the most beautiful picture in the world! I can't describe it. Like paradise. You must come by in the daytime and see it. Oh! Look, look!'

'Shhh! Don't shout like that, stupid! Some bastard will hear you for sure. What is it?'

Speechless, Kushi points behind Tabu's head. He turns, his hands still on her breasts. The headlights of passing cars are illuminating the fluorescent advertisement so that the running couple pulses in and out of the darkness in a magic dance.

'Oh, it's an ad.'

'What does that mean? Isn't it just beautiful, the most beautiful picture in the world?'

'Yeah, it's nice. Now come down a little, just like this. Wonderful!'

'Tabu-da, why are they running?'

'Wha-? Oh, to catch the plane. Mmmm. Love you. Move like this, baby.'

'Are they going to go where that magic city is?'

'Mmmm. Yeah.'

'Tabu-da, where is that magic city?'

'Huh? Oh, maybe in England, maybe America. Keep moving like I showed you. Oh God!'

'Why did they put up that picture at our house?'

'Shh, be quiet, I love you so much, baby. Don't stop me now. You know I wouldn't hurt you. My sweet, sweet, girl, tomorrow I'll bring you something even nicer to eat, maybe some mutton cutlets. Ohhh. . . .'

Kushi keeps looking at the golden couple, running, running. Their pink faces mesmerize her. Even from here she can see the flash of their smiles. Tabu-da is making a funny sound, shivering all over like her brother Nobu does when he has the fever. Her own body feels strange, too, kind of like it's going to explode. But she can't move, can't take her eyes from the couple. They seem to be coming closer to her, floating almost above her head. Kushi knows that if she reaches out her hand, she will be able to touch the woman's lacy skirt.

Edited and translated from the Bengali by Chitra Divakaruni

American Tourist

Stupid of me to think you were salmon
flapping your fins to swim upstream.
You didn't catch the jet to London
to lay eggs. Insemination was your dream.

Your eyelids are shutters, they take quick snaps
by day, and timed exposures by night;
your walk is an arrow in flight;
your questions drip-drop from a leaky tap.

The fish is different: a flying arc, it dives
only to rise and float away,
writing its story as it moves
with no care for what's beyond its snout.

Its essence is silence before, and after,
the net drains it out of the water.
No force drives it to its source
as you're driven. Its life is water on its course.

translated from the Kannada by A. K. Ramanujan
using the poet's own English version

The Hyoid Bone*

who can tell what lies behind
that high collar and sequestered
smile? while you try to impress me
i imagine your voice unfettered.

not the rib cage holding a bird,
but some other filament of bone
seems our metaphor, cleft-stick or
greek letter, the form's homegrown.

you appear uncomprehending. i know
that is the easiest path. we share
so little, it is absurd to think
my fancies please you, or you care.

and yet those fangs, prehensile
gaze, that roughly sprouting hair,
make you the essence of the ape
i knew ages ago. he was my pair.

there was a bone in this throat,
a funny crook-shaped thing, it

---

* The hyoid bone: a small bone at the base of the throat. It supports the muscles of
the tongue, and is believed to have been crucially important in the evolution of
speech. Shaped like the Greek letter υ (hueidos), it is not attached to any other
bone.

let him speak. stories shimmered
in cave's half-light, i loved it.

no not him, nor your complacent
litany of triumphs. it. i loved
the way words escaped like smoke
and i cried because i was dumb.

but things have changed. my fire
glows. you are ashen, worn. now
both stand upright and exchange
barbs. only one, however, knows.

i was the scholar who discovered
a miracle in the anatomy text,
the only bone in the entire body
not tied to any other, unannexed.

freedom's territory deep within
an unassuming bit of cartilege,
it teaches us detachment. virtue
you, my love, cannot appreciate.

for you are the dull one this time
round. turning on an endless wheel
of talk, your early gift's forgotten.
*moksha.** in your bondage, my release.

---

* Moksha: This all important term in Hindu/Buddhist soteriology is often
   translated as 'liberation,' or 'liberation from earthly desires/woes,' although
   many would contend that such a translation remains inadequate.

Genderole[*]

Considerthefemalebodyyourmost
Basictextanddontforgetitsslokas |

Whatpalmleafmscandoforusitdoes
Therealgapsremainforwomentoclose |

Spacesbetweenwordspreservesenses
Intactbutweneedtomeetineverysense |

Comingtogetherisnoverbalmatter
Howeveroursagespraisepativrata |

Katavakantakasteputrasamsaroyam[**]
Ativavichitrawaswrittenformenbyaman |

Theworlddoesnotseemsostrangeseen
Throughgentlereyesnorwomensoalien |

---

[*] Genderole: The poem is written in the run-on graphemic style of the Sanskrit couplet, with no breaks between words, and a stroke at the end.

[**] *katava kanta kaste putra samsaroyam ativa vichitra*: who is your wife? who are your children? this world is exceedingly strange.

Nalinidalagatajalamatitaralamtadvat[*]
Jivanamatishayachapalamchangeability |

Isinthenatureofthingsandespecially
Femalesbutsankarayouoldmisogynisttellme |

Whatssocontemptibleaboutfleeting
Splendour?andwhileyouareaboutitthink |

Wehavewrungpoemsfromhouseholdtasks
Carryingwaterchildsorrowcanyoudoasmuch? |

Itmaybebeneathyoutopriseapartthisgimmick
Butrememberthethingawomanchangesbestishersex |

Opposingyouischildsplaybecauseyoufail
Torealizethisandwecanbeatyouatyourowngame |

Muchhardertoconvertourselveshaving
Laboredlongatbeingmenwepossessnothing |

MyworstfearissankarathathadIindeedbeenyou
Imightnotafterallhaveconceivedanythingnew |

---

[*] *nalini dala gata jalam ati taralam tadvat jivanam atishaya chapalam*: like water poised
delicately on a lotus petal so astonishingly elusive is life.

Hundru Falls, Ranchi

More people than water. Voices
Litter the air. Great outcrop
Of rock, tethered at one end
To the sun, at the other to none.

The spray gets everything, food,
Cigarette ends, durries, even
His father's thump-thumping boots.
Boy wants to find the water-line.

Its source. His mother smiles,
Abstracted, dreaming of romance,
She does not hear his words.
Already, the body is a far blur.

Rock shifts, retreats, dances,
No different from the water.
The chatter fades upstream,
Mist covers his eyes, his face.

He is not the sort of boy missed
Immediately. When the searchers
Find him, days later, it is hard
To tell whispering boy from river.

Sitakanta Mahapatra

Winter Morning, Mist

The sea was all around us that morning:
the waves, at doorstep
smiled contentedly at my offerings
of rice, coconuts and marigolds—
interest paid on its ancient debt.

How generous of the sea
to call at my door for its dues!
to remember an obscure name
in its unending ledgers.

The sea's garrisons
had annexed houses, streets and trees,
every single object was
immaculate with eternity.

The sun dragged itself from bed,
and the sea melted
into my cup of tea.
The familiar landscape burned
in awful insularity.

The memory of that unclaimed debt
remains a winter's dream.

Translated from the Oriya by B. K. Das

A Poem for Sriradha

Give him up, quickly.

How can he be contained
in a prison as small as your lifetime?
He is the breath of the forest,
the breath one can neither see nor hold,
the breath that, with a single touch,
dishevels the hair and the sari.

You've almost murdered his speech
and wrapped his mountain-blue body in brocades.
All you are waiting for is to burn his exquisite face someday
in the cremation fire.

Return him to me.

He is the sound of thunder that is heard like the flute's note.
He commands me to dance,
and I dance from birth to birth, from death to death.
Go, tell him someone has arrived with bleeding but restless feet.
And, if he still does not respond, show him
this remainder of my life.

He may not have told you, but I am his bride.
Go, tell him at once.
He will surely come out—like the answer
to a question that has not been asked.

You will find where he used to sit
an ageing king wrapped up in brocades.
He will answer all your questions
in a language you will comprehend.

Translated from the Oriya by the poet

A Love Poem

What are you? I think you are
pure movement, and nothing but movement.
Sometimes, it is true, I see you draped in a sari
but, oftener, you are a disembodied impatience,
an invisible ship voyaging with a hurricane's speed
across an invisible ocean throughout the day and night
with a cargo of stifled words.

I could not see you, for the gale had blown away
my eyes, and my words were lost
somewhere in your embrace.
I was speechless and could not give the world
the details of what you were.
The streets, as usual, teemed with people.
There were, as usual, flowers in the garden.
Stars, as usual, thronged the whole sky.
But you, who are movement and nothing but movement
were, as usual, to be found nowhere.

And yet I know that I always exist
on the shaded banks of a fountain
somewhere within you.

Translated from the Oriya by the poet

Bone of Time

Is this why one always remembers:
the autumn night struggling with its breath,
the fireflies pulsing and drawing back
to reveal the fallen teeth of the jungle;
and the moon, to whom we owe
the tempests of light among the shadows,
seeking refuge
in a narrow window of our wakefulness.
The last time I saw you, I told myself:
I would see nothing, never again;
and the evening stars that fall to earth
can make the distance between us no shorter.
Your window looks so warm from here,
and the wind drifts away noiselessly
across the comfortless river;
bone of time
that makes each one understand
how night is night; and through it
to enter the kingdom where Orion turns,
calm and certain, into neither darkness nor light.

Khagama

We were eating dinner by the light of the petromax lamp, and I had just taken my first bite of curried egg when Lachman the watchman asked, 'Aren't you gentlemen going to have your *darshan** of Imli Baba?'

I was forced to confess that Imli Baba's name was unknown to us, so the question of an audience with him did not even arise. Lachman said that the driver of the Forest Department jeep which was reserved for us could take us to Baba's dwelling, if we asked. His hut was far into the jungle in a pleasant spot. As a holy man Baba was quite well-known; important people from all over India come to see him. Moreover, what made me most curious was the fact that Baba was supposed to have a pet king cobra which lived in a hole near his hut and came out to him every evening to drink goat's milk.

After hearing all of this, Dhurjati Babu remarked that the country was being overrun by charlatans, and especially fake holy men. Their number was dangerously high, and growing. The more the influence of science grew in the West, the more our country turned again to the darkness of superstition. 'A hopeless affair, sir! One gets apoplectic just thinking about it.'

Having said this, Dhurjati Babu put down his fork and spoon, picked up the fly swatter and with unerring aim killed a mosquito that had alighted on the table. Dhurjati Babu's age was between forty-five and fifty. He was short, lean, fair-skinned, with sharp features and very light, sand-coloured eyes. I had met him at

---

* Darshan: seeing a holy man or a deity.

Bharatpur. I had come through Agra; I was on my way to Jaipur to visit my second-eldest brother and to spend a fortnight's holiday there. Finding no room either at the *dak* bungalow or the tourist lodge, I had finally found a place to stay in the forest rest house. I did not regret this, since there was a kind of comfortable thrill in staying at the rest house, surrounded by the forest.

Dhurjati Babu had arrived a day ahead of me. What he had come for he had not yet disclosed to me, although there need have been no reason beyond simple sightseeing. We had been travelling around in the same jeep. Yesterday we had gone to a place twenty-two miles to the east, called Deeg, to see the fort and palace there. We had done Bharatpur Fort this morning and in the afternoon had gone to the bird sanctuary in the Keoladeo marsh. What a strange place! A lake over seven miles long, with banks like small islands raising their tops every so often. And every kind of bird in the world seemed to have gathered on those shoals, more than half of them species I had never even seen before. I watched the birds with astonishment, and Dhurjati Babu intermittently grumbled and restlessly waved his arms about in an attempt to drive the *unki* away from his face. *Unki* are a sort of small insect. They hover around your head in swarms and settle on your face. But they are so small that one could easily ignore them; but Dhurjati Babu, I observed, became irritated again and again. Such impatience!

About half-past-eight dinner was over, and as we sat on the front veranda on cane chairs and took in the beauty of the forest in the moonlight, I asked Dhurjati Babu, 'That *sadhu baba** we just heard about—would you care to go see him?'

Dhurjati Babu flicked the cigarette in his hand at the trunk of a eucalyptus tree and said, 'King cobras are never tame; they just cannot be tamed. I know about snakes. As a boy I lived in Jalpaiguri and I have killed any number of snakes with my own hands. The king cobra is a vicious, devilish snake, impossible to tame. I have my doubts about what we heard about our holy man.'

I said, 'Anyway, we have no plans for tomorrow afternoon. After we've visited the fort at Bayan in the morning, we're free.'

---

* Sadhu baba: a holy man.

'You have a lot of faith in holy men, do you?' I could sense the barb behind the question. But my reply was quite straightforward.

'Well, the question of faith doesn't quite arise, since I have never yet had the opportunity of the company of saints. But a certain curiosity; yes, that I don't deny.'

'I too had it once, but after my experience . . .'

His experience turned out to be this: Dhurjati Babu, it seems, suffered from high blood pressure. About ten years ago, persuaded by his father's elder brother, he had taken some quack medicine given by a *sadhu baba* and suffered unbearable pain for a week. As a result his blood pressure had shot up even more. Since then he had held the idea that ninety out of a hundred Indian holy men were really charlatans and frauds.

The man's '*baba*-baiting' was amusing, and to provoke him, I said, 'With regard to what you say about taming cobras, you and I may not be able to do it, but I've heard that some of the holy men of the Himalayas live with tigers right in the tigers' caves.'

'Sure you've heard that, but have you ever seen it?'

I had to admit, of course, that I had not.

'And you won't. This is a land of fantastic tales. You will hear about a lot of things, but ask for hard evidence and you will get to see nothing. Consider the *Ramayana* and the *Mahabharata*. They are called histories, but in reality they are just collections of weird tales. Ravana and his ten heads, Hanumana setting fire to Lanka with his burning tail, Bhima's appetite, Ghatotkacha, Hidimba, the Pushpaka chariot, Kumbhakarna—what is more nonsensical than all this? Speak of charlatans posing as holy men! It all begins with those Puranas. Yet the entire country—educated or not—has been swallowing it whole for all this time!'

*

It was four in the afternoon by the time we arrived at Imli Baba's hut, after seeing the fort at Bayan and a rest after lunch. Dhurjati Babu had raised no further objections in this matter. Perhaps he too was a little curious about Baba. Baba's hut was in a spacious open clearing under an *imli* or tamarind tree deep inside the jungle. Baba's name came from the tree; *imli* the local people had named him. No one knew Baba's real name.

Inside the hut made of date-palm fronds, attended by a single disciple, Baba was seated upon a bear skin. The disciple was young, but it was quite impossible to guess Baba's age. It was still an hour before sunset, but the place was already quite dark because of the dense cover of tamarind leaves. A small fire burned in front of the hut; there was a clay pipe of ganja in Baba's hand. By the light of the fire I saw a clothesline strung out on one side of the hut. Hanging from it was a cotton washcloth, a loincloth, and about ten sloughed snake skins.

Seeing us, Baba gave us a small smile from behind his pipe. Dhurjati Babu whispered, 'Get to the point without wasting time. Find out when the cobra comes for his milk.'

'You wish to meet Balkisan?'

Imli Baba had read our minds by some mysterious means. Deendayal, the driver of our jeep, had told us a short while ago that the king cobra was called Balkisan. We told Imli Baba that we had heard of his snake and were very eager to see the pet snake drink milk. Would we be so fortunate?

Imli Baba shook his head in an expression of regret. He said that every day at sunset Balkisan heard Baba's call and came out of his hole to the hut to drink milk, and had indeed done so two days back; but for the past day the snake had not been feeling too well. Since it was the day of the full moon, he would not be coming today either. He would come again tomorrow.

It was news to me that snakes could feel indisposed. But why not? It was a pet. After all, there were hospitals for cows, horses, dogs and the like.

The disciple gave us some more information. Not only was Balkisan not feeling well, but some carpenter ants had attacked him in his den and annoyed him. Baba's curse had, so the disciple said, blasted those ants to the five elements. At this Dhurjati Babu glanced at me out of the corners of his eyes. But I was looking at Imli Baba. There was nothing very distinctive in his appearance. He was dressed in a long loose ocher shirt. The hair on his head was matted but not very much. He had a pair of iron rings on his ears, about four or so necklaces of different sizes around his neck, and an amulet above his right elbow. His appearance was not too different from most 'holy men.' Nevertheless, in the failing light of that evening, I could not take my eyes off the man who sat behind the small fire. As we remained standing the disciple brought out a pair of reed mats and spread them out about ten paces from Baba. But since Baba's pet cobra was not to be seen, there was no point in sitting down. Delay would mean driving back in the dark. True, the car was there, but the road was through the jungle, and there was no dearth of wild animals around. We had seen herds of deer every day. So finally we did not sit down. As we saluted Baba, he returned our salute bowing his head with closed eyes, but without removing the clay pipe from his lips. The two of us started off for the jeep, which was parked on the road a hundred yards or so away. Just a short while back we could hear the tumultuous noise of birds coming home to roost in the surrounding trees; now all was quiet.

We had only gone a few paces from the hut when Dhurjati Babu suddenly stopped and said, 'Well, even if we could not see the snake, couldn't we at least have asked to see the hole it lives in?'

I replied, 'We don't have to go to Imli Baba for that. Our driver, Deendayal, said that he has seen the hole.'

'Quite right.'

We fetched Deendayal from the car and came back. This time we did not go towards the hut, but went down a narrow path past a nut tree till we came upon a thorn bush. The broken pieces of stone lying all around suggested that at one time there probably had been some kind of a structure here. Deendayal said that the snake's hole was directly behind the bush. There was no way to tell for sure since the light had become even more faint. Dhurjati Babu produced a small flashlight from his pocket, and as soon as the beam of light hit the bush, we saw the hole behind it. Well, at any rate, the hole really existed. But the snake? Would it come out, ill as it was, to satisfy our curiosity? To tell the truth, though I had wanted to see the king cobra drink milk from the *sadhu baba's* hand, I had no great desire to stand outside the hole of that same cobra for a *darshan*. But Dhurjati Babu's curiosity, I observed, was even greater than mine. When the beam of light failed to produce results, the man began to pelt the bush with clods of dirt. This excessive behaviour did not please me. 'What are you up to, sir?' I exclaimed. 'You are being mulish. And you wouldn't believe that there even was a snake.'

The man then picked up a fairly large clod in his hands and said, 'I don't now either. If this does not produce results, we'll know that the fantastic story spread about our holy man is a complete fraud. The more of these superstitions we can dispel, the better off we will all be.'

The lump of earth fell on the bush with a heavy thudding sound and shattered the leaves and thorns. Dhurjati Babu held the flashlight on the hole. For a few moments all was quiet—except that somewhere in the jungle a cricket started to chirp. Now another sound was added. A sound like a dry tuneless whistle. Then a rustle of leaves. Then a length of some smooth black object could be seen in the beam of the flashlight. It moved, it was alive, and gradually it emerged from the hole.

Now the leaves on the bush moved, and the next instant through the gap the head of a snake came out. In that beam of light I saw the blazing cobra eyes and its forked tongue that flickered out of its mouth again and again, quivered and slid back. Deendayal had been insistent about returning to the jeep for some time, and now he pleaded in a choking voice, 'Please, sir, let it be! Now that you've seen it, let's go back now.'

It was probably because of the beam of light that Balkisan still kept his head out and stared at us, and intermittently moved his tongue. I have seen many snakes, but I had never seen a deadly king cobra like this from so close. And a cobra looking on quietly, without moving to attack or flee. This too I had never seen. Suddenly the beam of light faltered and moved off from the snake. I was not at all ready for what took place next. Dhurjati Babu suddenly picked up a piece of stone and, in a flash, had hurled it aimed at Balkisan's head; he hurled two more in quick succession. Dazed by a horrible fear, I exclaimed, 'What are you doing, Dhurjati Babu!'

The man stood next to me panting loudly and said in a low voice with suppressed jubilation, 'One cobra less!'

Deendayal stared at the bush, eyes dilated, mouth open. Taking the flashlight from Dhurjati Babu I turned the beam on the hole. A portion of Balkisan's inert body was visible. The leaves of the bush were stained with blood spattered from the snake's head.

During all of this I had not noticed that Imli Baba and his disciple had come up and now stood behind us. Dhurjati Babu was the first to turn around. Then I too turned around to see Baba, staff in hand, standing under a dwarfish date tree about ten paces away from us, and staring fixedly at Dhurjati Babu. Having only seen him seated, I had failed to notice how tall he really was. And the look in his eyes is beyond my powers of description. I can only say this: I had never seen such a combined look of surprise, anger and hatred in anyone's eyes.

Now Baba's right arm came up in front. He pointed at Dhurjati Babu. The index finger came out and the direction was clear. For the first time I saw that each nail on Baba's fingers was nearly two inches long. Who was I reminded of as I looked at Baba? A painting by Ravi Varma, a memory from my childhood on the wall in my uncle's house on Beadon Street. The ascetic Durvasa cursing Shakuntala. Arm raised in just this way, the same look in the eyes.

But Imli Baba made no curses. In his solemn low voice, what he said in Hindi was this: What if one Balkisan is gone? Another will come. There is no death for Balkisan. Balkisan is immortal.

Dhurjati Babu wiped his dusty hands on a handkerchief, turned towards me and said, 'Let's go.' The disciple came and removed the dead cobra from the mouth of the hole, probably to arrange its funeral. An expression of amazement involuntarily escaped my lips when I saw its length. I had no idea that a king cobra could be that long. Imli Baba returned slowly to his hut. The three of us went and got into the jeep.

On the road back to the rest house, seeing Dhurjati Babu sitting glumly, I could not help making a remark. I said, 'Since the snake was that man's pet and was causing you no harm, why did you have to kill it?'

I had expected that the fellow would make further pronouncements about snakes and *sadhus* and try to support his malicious act. But he did none of that, and asked me a completely irrelevant question instead, 'Khagama, tell me, who is Khagama?'

Khagama? The name seemed vaguely familiar, but I could not remember where I had heard or read it. Dhurjati Babu muttered

'Khagama' to himself a couple of more times and finally fell silent. When we reached the rest house it was half-past-six. I kept remembering the way Imli Baba appeared—like Durvasa, eyes red, hand pointing at Dhurjati Babu. Who could explain the man's folly. But in my mind I thought that we had seen the end of the affair, so there was no point in brooding about it anymore. Baba had himself said that Balkisan was immortal. Were there no more king cobras in the Bharatpur jungle? By tomorrow, surely, Baba's disciples would catch another cobra and present it to him.

For dinner Lachman had cooked curried chicken, fresh bread fried in ghee, and *urad* lentils. After we had walked the whole day, appetites were naturally quite keen. With no effort at all I could eat twice what I would eat for dinner in Calcutta. Dhurjati Babu was small and slightly built, but nevertheless had quite a capacity for food. But tonight it seemed the man had lost his appetite. When I asked if he felt ill, he made no reply. I said, 'Are you feeling sorry about Balkisan?'

Dhurjati Babu did say something at this but it could hardly be called an answer to my question. Looking fixedly at the petromax, in a voice which was very soft and thin he said, 'The snake was whispering. The snake . . . was . . . whispering.'

I replied, smiling, 'Whispering, or hissing?'

Dhurjati Babu shook his head without moving his eyes away from the light, 'No, it was whispering. Snake speech is whistle, whisper, lisp . . .'

Saying this he himself made a sound through his teeth, like the whistling of a snake, several times. Then, swaying his head he rhymed, 'Snakes whistle, snakes lisp, snakes whisper, whistle, lisp! His voice is poison, whistle, lisp, snakes whisper, whistle, lisp! . . . What's this? Goat milk?'

The last, of course, was not part of the rhyme. It was addressed to the pudding on the plate.

Lachman understood the 'milk,' but without understanding the 'goat' part said, 'Yes, sir, there's milk in it, and eggs too.' Everyone knows, of course, that milk and eggs go into making a pudding.

Dhurjati Babu was normally an eccentric, freakish sort of fellow, but his manner today struck me as being a bit excessive.

Possibly he himself sensed this, for he appeared to get a grip on himself and said, 'Out in the sun too much the last few days. Probably that's why my head . . . must be a little more careful from now on.'

The night became quite chilly, so after dinner, instead of sitting outside, I went to my room to pack my bag. I would leave Bharatpur on the evening train tomorrow. Change trains at midnight at Sawai Madhopur and arrive at Jaipur early in the morning at five.

*

At least that was my plan. But that plan came to nothing. I had to wire my second-eldest brother to inform him that because of unavoidable circumstances my departure had to be postponed by a day. I will now relate how that came to pass. I will try to relate the incidents as clearly and as exactly as possible. That everyone will not believe this happened, I know very well. The one thing that could have been my proof is probably lying on the ground fifty paces north of Imli Baba's hut. The mere thought of it makes me shiver, so is it surprising that I could not pick it up with my hands and bring it as proof? Let that pass—let's get to the incidents.

After packing my bag, turning down the lantern and placing it behind the dressing table, changing into my nightclothes, I was about to climb into bed when there was a knock on the door on the east side of the room. Dhurjati Babu's room was behind this door.

As soon as I opened the door the man said in a low subdued sort of voice, 'Do you have any kind of mosquito repellent or insect spray with you?'

I said, 'How did the mosquitoes get in? Aren't the doors and windows of your room screened?'

'Yes, they are.'

'Well, then?'

'Nevertheless, something is biting me.'

'Can you feel it?'

'My skin is covered with marks.'

It was dark in front of the door, so I could not make him out very clearly. I said, 'Come inside. Let me see these marks.'

Dhurjati Babu came into the room. As soon as I lifted up the light I saw the marks. Diamond-shaped bruises. I had never seen this before, and what I saw did not please me at all. I said, 'You've got some weird infection. It may be from an allergy. We'll have to look for a doctor first thing tomorrow morning. Try to get some sleep. Don't fret about it now. And this isn't from an insect, it's something else. Does it hurt?'

'No.'

'At least that's good. Go, lie down.'

He went off, and I climbed into bed and slipped under the blanket. It is my habit to read in bed, but that was not possible here by the light of the lantern. Not that it was really necessary. After the day's tiring activities sleep would come within ten minutes of putting my head down on the pillow.

But that did not happen tonight. My drowsiness was interrupted by the sound of a motor car. I could hear an English voice and the bark of a strange dog. Some tourists arriving at the rest house. Someone scolded the dog, and it stopped barking. The visitors must have turned in. Again everything was quiet. Only the cicadas calling outside! No, not just the cicadas. I heard another sound. My neighbour on the east side was still awake. Not only awake but moving about. I heard his footsteps. Yet through the crack under the door, I had seen a short while ago that the lantern was either put out or left in the bathroom next door. Why was the man pacing about in a dark room?

It was then I first suspected that Dhurjati Babu was more than just a little odd in the head. I had only known him for a couple of days. I did not know anything about him beyond what he himself had told me. But to be honest, till just a few hours ago I had seen no signs in him of what could be called insanity. The sort of remarks he made while touring the forts of Deeg and Bayan gave the impression that he had read history quite well. Not only that. In his conversation he had given proof of a fair grasp of art history. He had spoken with enthusiasm of the work of Hindu and Muslim craftsmen in the architecture of Rajasthan. No—the man was physically ill. It was essential to look for a doctor tomorrow.

The radium dial of my watch said a quarter-to-eleven. There was another rap on the east side door. This time, without getting up from bed, I shouted, 'What's the matter, Dhurjati Babu?'

'S-s-s-s- . . .'

'What's that you say?'

'S-s-s-s- . . .'

I gathered the man was having difficulty with his speech. This was one fine mess I had got myself into! I said again, 'Can you say that a little more clearly?'

'S-s-s-say, can you come here a moment?'

I was forced to get up. When I opened the door, the man asked such an odd question that I was quite annoyed. 'Is s-s-snake spelt with a dental s?'

I made no attempt to hide my irritation. 'You knocked on the door this late at night with a question like this?'

'Is it a dental s?'

'Yes, sir. When *sapa* means "serpent, snake," it's a dental s.'

'And the palatal *sh*?'

'That's a different *shapa*. It means . . .'

'. . . *abhishapa*, "curse"?'

'Yes, a curse.'

'Thank you. Please go back to s-s-sleep.'

Seeing the state the man was in, I was somewhat moved to being charitable. I said, 'Why don't I give you a sleeping pill! I have them with me. Want one?'

'No. I s-s-sleep in winter, anyway. Only at s-s-suns-s-set, in the evening-s-s-s . . .'

I interrupted the man and said, 'Is there something the matter with your tongue? Why do you have difficulty talking? Here, give me your flashlight for a moment.'

I went into his room behind him. The flashlight was on his dressing table. As soon as I pressed it on and turned it on his face he opened his mouth and stuck out his tongue. There was no doubt there was something wrong with his tongue. A thin red line started at the tip and ran all the way to the middle of the tongue.

'And this isn't hurting either?'

'Well, no.'

I could not imagine what the man had caught.

Now my eyes moved to his bed. I gathered from its tidiness that so far he had not been in bed at all. In a fairly stern voice I said,

'I'll return to my room only after I've put you to bed. And I beg you with joined hands—please, please, don't knock on my door again. I know that there'll be no sleeping on the train tomorrow, so I want to get some sleep tonight.'

But the man showed no interest in going to bed. The lantern was in the bathroom so there was no light in the room to speak of. There was a full moon outside; through the window on the north, moonlight came in and fell on the floor. By its reflected light I could make out Dhurjati Babu, standing there in his nightclothes and intermittently parting his lips to make a noise like whistling. I had put the blanket around me when coming, but Dhurjati Babu stood there, doing quite well without anything warm around him. If the man ultimately got sick with a serious disease, it would be really difficult for me to leave. One Bengali falls ill in a strange and foreign place, and another sneaks off without doing anything for him—that could hardly be allowed to happen.

When my repeated request for him to get to bed proved fruitless, I understood that there was nothing else to be done but to take him by the hand and forcibly put him to bed. If he wanted to be a disobedient child, I was forced to play the role of the strict parent.

But as soon as I took hold of his hand, I had such a physical reaction that, startled, I jumped back three paces.

Dhurjati Babu's body was as cold as ice. I could never have imagined that the body of a living person could be this cold.

It was probably the state I was in that brought a smile to the corners of his mouth. He smiled faintly, regarding me with his tawny eyes. In a hoarse voice, I asked, 'What's the matter with you?'

Dhurjati Babu did not remove his eyes from me. For a whole minute he stared at me fixedly. Speechless from shock, I saw that his eyes did not blink at all. In the meantime his tongue flickered out from between his lips again and again. Then, in a voice reduced to a whisper, he said, 'Baba is calling, "Balkisan! Balkisan!" . . . Baba is calling . . .'

Then his knees folded. First he knelt down. Then thrusting his body forward, he lay prone on the ground, put his weight on his elbows and dragging himself, disappeared into the darkness under the bed.

I could distinctly feel my whole body wet with perspiration, my limbs knocking against each other. I could not keep standing up anymore. My anxiety for the man had disappeared, and what I now felt was a strange horrible feeling made up of disbelief and terror.

I came back to my room.

Closing the door and bolting it, I wrapped myself in the blanket and lay down for a while; my shivering stopped, my mind cleared. I thought about what was happening, what I had seen happen with my own eyes, and what conclusions could be drawn from it. This afternoon, before my eyes, Dhurjati Babu killed Imli Baba's pet cobra with a blow from a stone. Right after that, Imli Baba pointed a finger at Dhurjati Babu and said, one Balkisan is gone, another Balkisan will come in its place. That second Balkisan, was it a snake or a man?

Or was it a man-turned-snake?

What were the welts all over Dhurjati Babu's body?

What was the red line on his tongue? Was it the stage preceding its splitting in two?

Why was his body so cold?

Instead of lying down on the bed, why did he crawl under it?

Suddenly something came back to me like a flash of lightning. Khagama! Dhurjati Babu was asking about Khagama. The name had seemed familiar, but I couldn't quite place it. But now I remembered the story from the *Mahabharata* read in childhood. There was an ascetic named Khagama. Because of his curse his friend, the sage Sahasrapada, had become a poisonless snake. Khagama *sapa-shapa* . . . it all jibed. But that one had become a snake without poison, and this one . . . ?

Someone knocked on my door again. Not up above, but near the bottom of the door. Just above the threshold. Once, twice, three times. I did not move from the bed. I will not open the door. Not anymore!

The sound stops. I hold my breath and listen intently. Now the sound of whistling came to my ears. From near the door it gradually moved away. Now, no sound other than my heartbeat.

What was that? A high-pitched screeching. A thin, sharp scream. Was it a mouse? There were mice here. I had seen them in my room the first night. When I informed Lachman, he came from the kitchen the next day with a mouse trap and showed me a live mouse. 'There are not only mice here, but also moles,' he had said.

The cry gradually faded, to silence. Ten minutes passed. I looked at my watch. A quarter-to-one. Don't know where my sleepiness has vanished to. The foliage outside can be seen through the window. The moon was probably directly overhead.

The sound of a door being opened. In the next room Dhurjati Babu has opened the door to the veranda. The side of my room with the window also had a door to the veranda. It was similar to Dhurjati Babu's room. Down from the veranda, twenty steps away, the vegetation began.

Dhurjati Babu came out onto the veranda. Where was he going off to? What were his intentions? I stared fixedly at the window.

I heard the sound of whistling. It gradually became louder. Now it was right outside my window. Lucky the window has a wire mesh screen, or . . .

Something is rising upwards from below the window. It stops after a while. A head. In the faint light of the lantern a pair of burning, tawny eyes. The eyes look at me with a lidless stare.

After remaining like this for a whole minute, as soon as it hears the bark of a dog, the head turns to the left and the next instant goes down again and disappears from sight.

The dog barks. It is desperately howling for help. Then I hear a sleepy voice telling it in English to shut up. With an anguished groan, the dog falls silent. Then, no more sound. For about ten minutes I lay there with all my senses alert. Repeatedly, a rhyme heard this evening comes back to me:

> *Snakes whistle, snakes lisp*
> *Snakes whistle, whisper, lisp*
> *His voice is poison, whistle, lisp*
> *Snakes whistle, whisper, lisp*

Slowly the rhyme too faded. I could feel a pulsing, drowsy, exhaustion pulling me under, towards sleep.

*

I woke up to the hubbub of English voices. I looked at my watch—it was ten to six. Something was wrong. Getting up hurriedly I put on something warm and found the fair-skinned visitors outside. Two young men, Americans—Bruce and Michael were their names—their pet dog had died the night before. They had gone to bed with the dog inside the room but had not locked their door. They suspected that it all happened in the night from the bite of a scorpion or snake—something with venom. Michael thought it was a scorpion since it is well known that snakes do not come out in the winter.

Without wasting any time on the dog I went towards Dhurjati Babu's room at the other end of the veranda. The door was open, but he was not in the room. Lachman got up daily at half-past-five in the morning and lighted the stove to make hot water for tea. When asked, he said that he had not seen Dhurjati Babu.

Many kinds of fearful speculations tumbled through my mind. I had to find the man by whatever means possible. How far could he have gone on foot? But no trace of him could be found after searching all around the forest.

The jeep arrived at half-past-ten. I told the driver that I had to go to the post office; there was a telegram to send to Jaipur. I could not leave Bharatpur without solving the mystery of Dhurjati Babu.

After sending the telegram to my second-eldest brother and changing my train ticket to the next day, I came back to the rest house to learn that even then there was no news of Dhurjati Babu. The two Americans had buried their dog and vanished with their bags.

All through midday I wandered around the rest house. The jeep returned, as I had asked, in the afternoon. There was a plan in my head, something in my mind said it might work. I told the driver, 'Let's go to Imli Baba.'

I reached Baba's hut at about the same time as the day before. As before, Baba was seated behind his lighted fire. Today there were two more disciples, one of middle age and the other a young fellow.

As soon as he saw me Baba lowered his head in greeting. His gaze today had no likeness to the withering gaze of yesterday. Without wasting any time I directly asked him if he could give me any news of the gentleman who had come with me yesterday. A sympathetic smile filled Baba's face. He said, 'Indeed, there is news. Your friend has fulfilled my hope; he has brought my Balkisan back again.'

For the first time I noticed the black stone bowl kept at Baba's right hand. The white liquid in it was nothing but milk. But I had not come this far to see a snake and a milk bowl. I had come in the quest of Dhurjatiprasad Basu. The man could not have disappeared into thin air. If I could see even a single sign of his existence, I could at least feel a little less distraught.

I had seen before that Imli Baba could read people's minds. After a hard pull on the pipe of ganja, he passed it on to the middle-aged disciple next to him and said, 'Of course, you won't get back your friend as he was before, but he has left behind a memento. That you will find fifty paces south of Balkisan's nest. Go carefully; there are many thorn trees in the way.'

I went near Balkisan's hole as Baba had suggested. I did not have the slightest curiosity to know if there was a snake in there or not. I looked at the setting sun in the sky and measured off to the south. Counting off fifty paces through grass, thornbush, broken stones and prickly thistle, I went forward and found something by the trunk of an *arjun* tree the likes of which I had seen hanging from a line in Imli Baba's hut a few minutes back.

It was a sloughed-off skin. All over the skin was a pattern of diamonds.

But was it a snake's? No, it was not. Is a snake's body ever this wide? And does it grow a pair of arms on the sides and a pair of legs below?

In fact, it was the sloughed-off skin of a man. But the man was not a man anymore. He is now lying coiled inside that hole. He is of the genus cobra; there is poison in his fangs.

There, his whistle has started. There, the sun has gone down. There, now, Imli Baba is calling.

'Balkisan . . . Balkisan . . . Balkisan . . . .'

Translated from the Bengali by Aditi Nath Sarkar

The Ritual of *Sati**

The dog has crossed the knee-deep dark
    stream of water,
that trickle oozing out of your eyes
    is your Baitarani River.
Your *jamrul*-tree body covered
    with poisonous ants,
a hard fist holds you down, in case you want
    to come back.
You're going to burn here, now mount
    the funeral pyre.
You're going to burn here, now mount
    the memory pyre.
You're going to burn here—bloody lips,
    navel the colour of copper.
Lift the face-cloth, take a last look
    at your husband's face.

Translated from the Bengali by Paramita Banerjee and Carolyne
Wright

---

* On 4 September 1987, in the Rajasthani village of Deorala, eighteen-year-old Roop Kanwar burned herself alive on her husband's funeral pyre. Eyewitnesses first claimed that the girl committed *sati* voluntarily, but later it emerged that her in-laws dragged her screaming to the pyre.

Tiger Mask Ritual
after a photograph by Raghubir Singh*

When you put on the mask the thunder starts.
Through the nostril's orange you can smell
the far hope of rain. Up in the Nilgiris
glisten of eucalyptus, drip of pine, spiders
tumbling from their silver webs.

The mask is raw and red as bark against your facebones.
You finger the stripes ridged like weals
out of your childhood. A wind is rising
in the north, a scarlet light
like a fire in the sky.

When you look through the eyeholes it is like falling.
Night gauzes you in black. You are blind
as the beginning. Sniff, seek the moon.
After a while you will know
that creased musky smell
is rising from your skin.

Once you locate the ears the drums begin.
Your fur stiffens. A roar from the distant left,
like monsoon water. The air

---

* The poem refers to an ancient custom of the Rajasthani hill tribes of India
  performed to ensure rain and a good harvest.

is hotter now and moving. You swivel
your sightless head.
Under your sheathed paw the ground shifts, wet.

A small wild sound is sheltering
in your skull
against the circle that always closes in
just before dawn.

Two Women Knitting

Rama said
Rama said to Uma
Oh my,
How time passes.
Ah me, says Uma
And then both fall silent.

The two women cast on stitches
Skip stitches, slip the skipped stitches over,
Knit over purl,
Purl over knit.
After many intricate loops and cables
Their dark secrets still lie locked within
They have thrown the keys to their jewel casques in the lake.
Put the keys in, and their locks will bleed real blood.

Two women are knitting
Clicking steel against steel
Passersby look up amazed at the sparks that fly.
Loneliness comes at every other row in their patterns
Though they have worn each others' saris
And bathed each others' slippery infants
Even though at this very moment their husbands
Lie asleep in the rooms upstairs
Shaking them in their dreams.

Translated from the Hindi by Arlene Zide and the poet

Deciphering a Stone Inscription

As if I were deciphering a stone inscription,
I look at my mother.
In her eyes I see
the evening when the cattle return home.
Her days stand out
like bones when the skin is worn thin.

Coarse ropes twist in my innards.
I clasp the railing with both hands,
thinking of the waters
frozen between her and me.
A thousand railings light up,
and melt away.
There are winding steps,
circling around,
and falling down, down.
Steps.
And in each step are embedded
cow's eyes—wide open.

Translated from the Marathi by Vilas Sarang

The Art of Living

Each act of creation encompasses two crucial elements—a science and its practice as an art. Without one the other is incomplete: a science without practice is devoid of proof and a practice without science, of foundation. Therefore, every science harbours an element of practice and every practice succeeds by following its ground rules. For example, if one learns everything about primary and secondary colours and everything about various kinds of brushes but never tries to paint a picture, one's knowledge remains unexamined and therefore incomplete. Similarly, if one suddenly begins to fill in colours without any knowledge of paints and brushes, one fails. Thus, in order to succeed as a painter, one must first learn the science of painting and then put it into practice. The same is true of other arts.

A careful observation of our world reveals that human existence is an art. For personal and social development, knowledge of a certain science—some principles of conduct—is necessary. And equally necessary, if not more so, is the appropriate use of these principles at all times. Throughout our life if we carry principles that we cannot use, we are no different from an animal carting a load of weapons or scriptures. On the other hand, if we use our principles incorrectly, our practice is no more than the mantras squawked by a parrot.

However, the principles necessary for life are so embedded in our consciousness that they are unclear without an explanation of their use in practice. For instance, we know the maxim, '*satyam bruyat*,'* but we cannot improve ourselves or our society without practicing it in different situations. And we cannot practice it without internalizing its true spirit. Practice requires a grasp of the subtlety implicit in a principle.

India perhaps surpasses the world in her knowledge of principles, yet in our day-to-day life we often leave our principles untouched, like misers. This curse of not knowing the art of living is rampant across society. However, the woman is its chief victim.

In actuality, our ancients did not favour any individual at the cost of society. That their knowledge of life was individual as well as group oriented, specific as well as general, and unified as well as diverse is evident from the appeal their principles have to our unconscious minds. And that they used their principles correctly and progressively is evident from the way they constructed a healthy society to develop the whole being of the individual. But if for centuries we have dragged the same principles as dead weight, the fault is ours. If we wanted an energetic and active life, if we could determine the utility of principles by applying them to our specific circumstances, and if we had allowed the theory of knowledge to flow with its praxis, our life indeed would have been a model of high art. Instead, we turned away from right action, and thus turned the crucial principles of life into heavy shackles on our feet. Is it a wonder then that we, and especially women, feel frustrated?

Today, does the Indian woman lack a single virtue that can make her a model of humanity? She owns the farthest limit of tolerance that enables her to undertake a fire ordeal with a smile; she rushes into the loftiest sacrifice and destroys a man's small-minded meanness in an instant; and she embodies the god-like purity that guards the envied treasures of our culture. Even today, when women of enlightened countries are eagerly seeking physical comforts, she is a self-sacrificing mother, a devoted wife, a loving sister, and an obedient daughter. Even today, the poorest of men has at least one tolerant, sacrificing, loving woman in his ramshackle hut. But while she knows every

---

* *Satyam bruyat*: One should speak the truth.

aspect of love, self-sacrifice, and self-immolation, she knows nothing about the art of living, the art that empowers these other-worldly qualities.

How does a woman wrench her heart into a stone? To understand this phenomenon, observe the transformation of a baby girl into an accursed widow who crushes her most cherished desires for the sake of her deceased husband, subjects her body and mind to inhuman discipline, and dries her eyes lest tears pollute a relative of her deceased husband. Who will not marvel at the wife who bears the name of *ardhangini** yet enslaves her drunk, cruel, and sub-animal husband with her torn body and soul, and propitiates the gods to give her that very husband life after life? Who will not cry at the daughter who, at the unarticulated wish of her father, silently enshrouds the purple dreams of her youth and offers herself to the meanest among men? Who can believe that jealousy is a basic human emotion after watching the sister most affectionately tie a *rakhi* around the wrist of her brother drowned in her father's palatial luxuries, usurped from her so early in life? And who will fail to appreciate the adage, 'There was never a bad mother,' on seeing the mother's divine happiness for the cowardly son whose disrespect has wounded her a thousand times? After witnessing such untold tolerance, unspeakable sacrifice, and superhuman courage, the observer cannot but wonder, 'Are these women alive? Do they possess human consciousness?' And if they do not, what worth are their virtues? A corpse tolerates every insult peacefully—we can throw it to a crocodile, toss it in the air, or burn it on a pyre. It will neither sigh, nor cry, nor move. But can we praise its tolerance?

Today, the Indian woman is motionless like a corpse. An overabundance of principles restrains her from expressing her happiness or sorrow even if she wishes to. Moreover, after hearing unlimited praises for her limitless tolerance, she has come to perceive it as the essence of her being. Thus, the very principles that shape life into proportion and beauty have made her crooked and ugly. And now both her life and her principles are suffocating

---

* Ardhangini: one half of the body; the male and female together make one complete body in this taxonomy.

her like heavy woollens worn by a summer traveller.

Hindu society has done its best to preserve her solely as an exhibit of her ancient glory. Century after century has elapsed, bringing sharp currents of change. Yet the society which thrust slavery upon the woman has demanded from her the stability of a rock. Such stability can be an ornament for death, not for life. And while death has its own beauty, it can never fill the corridors of life.

Why woman is cherished as a rock may be explained by the powers of capital, religion, and authority. Monetary capital alone weighs more than religion and authority combined. Man obtained virtual mastery over capital by obtaining the responsibility for earning money. Then because of his greater physical strength he obtained easy authority. And by formulating social rules, he managed to keep himself more and more free and the woman more and more in bondage.

The enslaving machine, constructed with economic, religious, and social authority, became so effective that the woman molded in it emerged as a perfect slave. Lacking not an iota in her mental or physical slavery, she soon learned that to question her situation was to court punishment in life and hell in death. Today in the era of machines, the ingenuity of this ancient machine is awe-inspiring because the very product of this machine, a dumb sufferer, nullifies the work of her helper. It is believed that to save a person's humanity is a feat, but to destroy it so completely that the person regards her destruction to be the most precious, glorious, and vital gift is a marvel.

From her birth every girl begins to believe herself to be so much the object of another's possession that even a fleeting desire not to belong to that other is a sin to her. In the business of marriage, she must forget her education in order to equalize the two parties, and never develop her mind. Her capabilities and accomplishments must count as articles for her husband's exhibition and pride, not means to explore the truth, beauty, and goodness of her being. Virtues such as love, sensitivity, empathy, obedience, and purity must transform her in her husband's image, not contribute to any cause. She must neither choose an aim for her life nor quarrel with the constitution determined for her by society. Her life must be so dedicated to entertaining and procreating for her husband that she should have no need to use her heart or mind.

The above is not to say that the duties of a housewife are insignificant, provided they are accepted by the woman with volition and with accompanying rights. Her slavery can change into a coveted mastery if she has any rights other than food and shelter in the home that is the goal of her life since childhood, and if she has any say in the life of the man to whom her own is singularly devoted. Whose home is it on the threshold of which she cannot step without the prior permission of its master? And the husband whose worst oppression and lowliest behaviour she cannot resist without being branded a criminal? Should she consider them anything more than prison and prisoner?

There is no doubt that the woman has some responsibility for her condition. By merely carting the load of age-old principles, she has become a load for herself. By aiming at a mark above the human reach, a person reduces herself to a stone idol and by aiming below human heights, she becomes an animal. The first is the cessation of life; the second, a blemish on humanity. In none of these conditions can she reach her potential. In our society, the male, because of his selfishness, is a curse on humanity; and the female, because of her ignorant tolerance, is a neglected stone. Only when both of them become fully human can the art of living be realized, the art whose target is love fuelled by volition.

In order to achieve a beautiful and useful life, we will have to develop inner energy in accordance with our principles as well as the outer energy required to activate those principles. To take an example from nature, only a tree with energetic roots can stand unaided on the earth's surface and bear fruit in the face of repeated storms. Conversely, only a tree breathing fresh air above the earth can develop energetic roots. If the tree's outer energy turns inwards, it dies. Today, our spirituality claims to have conquered hell, but our day-to-day life is becoming deformed. The path of life does not merely traverse imaginary heavens, but also clears the thorny pathways of this world. Until our inner and outer energies draw from each other, we cannot live a beautiful life.

Edited and translated from the Hindi by Chandra Agrawal

The Night Has Come To An End

Night has come to an end, the woman starts her grinding.
Chants her *kohl*-darkened, sleep-filled couplet to the grindstone god.

Round and round goes her arm, down pours the flour.
Silent grief across her lap, quietly sucking its fist.

Whatever feelings she may have, those sweepings she brushes aside.
The woman empties her mind for the sake of home and hearth.

One ahead, one behind, life summons her.
The day ends, denying all of this, the day ends.

At dusk, waterpot braced by her hand, the mother
Bears the burden of children and menfolk on her head.

One waterpot, one *dudi* above the other, the woman comes
                                    toward the water.
Not toward the water, but comes to her childhood home.

The water gently sways, the dream enters the water, drowns.
When the moon enters the song, every day she asks for death,
        The woman asks for death.

Translated from the Marathi by Asha Mundlay and Arlene Zide

one after another after another

beside me, the lake's fire
my mind cannot say a thing
still water,
above it, fire chirping
like a bird
and there, the flaming noon

so many burning accidents
are rooted in calm
but dirty water

the mind won't say anything
yet it's not so calm
as to remain silent

even though
one gravelly dawn's gravel light
doesn't give a glimpse of morning
to any eye,
it has the light's fluid anger

accidents with fire
one after another after another

stuck in a noose, face
smothered in a black cowl
as if talking to itself
for the first time, the mind

one after another after another
reflected images cut through earlier ones
nothing stays
or else, so many reflections
remain, glimmer
like a fuss of raindrops
clinging to electric wires

then
disappear
one after another after another

Translated from the Hindi by Aditya Behl

The Girl's Desire among the Bangles

The girl's desire moves among the bangles
They should break, first, upon his bed
Then break upon the threshold of his house.*

But why upon the threshold?

Because within the girl, sits a forlorn woman
A woman who's a widow
Oh, not really
But surely one who'll become
A widow.

The girl's fear throbs within her veins
And moves across her bangles
The girl's desire throbs within them
They throb with her sorrow.

Sorrow?

Where is this girl's man?
The man in her mourning veins
Who fills her bangles with desire?

---

* When a woman becomes a widow, she ceremoniously breaks in a single violent
  act of desperation the glass bangles which she has worn as a sign of marriage.

Her man lies caught
In someone else's body
In someone else's dream, someone else's sorrow.
Someone else's tears.
Every one of his sorrows, his dreams, his tears
Are beyond the girl's mourning grasp.

But the girl is still a girl
The same primitive innocence in her
Fills her with madness, a deathwish
For which, evermore, she will punish
In days to come, the man.
When she will smash her bangles
On the threshold of his house. . . .

Translated from the Hindi by Mrinal Pande and Arlene Zide

Ghazal

The pure pain with which he recognizes angels
has left him without cures among the dreamless angels.

The dawn looked over its shoulder to ask the naked night
for the new fashions in which it could dress angels.

Is it that I've been searching in the wrong places for you?
That your address is still Los Angeles, Angels?

The air is my vinegar, I, its perfect preserve—
Watch how I'm envied by Heaven's meticulous angels.

In Inferno the walls mirror brocades and silks—
Satan's legions—though fallen—are, nonetheless, angels.

'Let there be Light,' He said. 'And the music of the spheres.'
To what tune does one set *The Satanic Verses*, Angels?

I won't lift, off the air, any wingprints, O God—
Hire raw detectives to track down the mutinous angels.

All day we call it wisdom but then again at night
it's only pain as it comes from the darkness, Angels!

Do they dye their wings, after Forever, tinting their haloes,
ageing zero without Time, those androgynous angels?

You play innocence so well, with such precision, Shahid:
You could seduce God Himself and fuck the sexless angels.

The Whirligig of Time

Dr Vachaspati Sharma lay slumped on the sofa. In the kitchen, his devoutly-wedded wife Savitri Sharma was seasoning with hot ghee and spices a vegetable dish made of the green leaves of the mustard plant. Before him the TV was on. In their house the TV was never switched off until the last member of the family had gone to bed. When friends dropped in its volume was turned down. Dr Sharma never cared which programme was on. With a flick of the button on his TV, he could bring flocking into his drawing-room all those objects of the American society which he had secretly in his past regarded, or did even now regard, as worth attaining and which he had not yet attained. After forty years of his life had gone by it was an unpleasant truth which he feared to acknowledge that the fair white girl who crooned on the TV to advertise toothpaste would probably never come into his life now. His elder daughter Munni was now going on fifteen. What a change from the time when he had first come to America as a student.

Back in Banaras he had seen roaming about on the Dashashwamedh Ghat by the Ganges barefoot and half-naked young men and women from the West—all of whom he had believed to be Americans. At times Sharmaji's heart would leap up uncontrollably on seeing the half-ripe bulging breasts of those girls. He had also seen some American films. He never was to see films like those again once he had arrived in America. But the freedom of the man-woman relationship depicted in those films had made a deep impact on him. A repressive society and an orthodox Hindu family had held his fleshly desires in strict check. It was then that he had decided that he would go to America for further studies.

He had begun to dream of his future in America occasionally—sometimes during the day and sometimes at night.

Dr Vachaspati Sharma had been born and brought up in the Chhapra district of the state of Bihar. After passing high school he had gone to the local degree college and got his B. Sc. It had been the wish of his father Pandit Balmukunda Sharma that his only son should turn out to be a famous academic. Therefore Vachaspati was sent off to do an M. Sc. at the Banaras Hindu University. He was admitted there to the Department of Physics. After Chhapra even Banaras seemed a new world. His heart would bloom and his fancy take wing at the sight of four or five girls coming to the university hoisted and laden all on the same rickshaw. All to himself he would compare and contrast three kinds of girls.

The first kind was represented by Savitri, the daughter of the village priest Pandit Shivashambhu Prasad Trivedi, to whom Vachaspati's family had sometime ago had him betrothed; he couldn't even honestly recall what she looked like. It had been his father's decision that he should be got engaged before he went off to study at Banaras. His only recollections of Savitri were from early childhood. In the summer season all the children of the village would gather to play in the mango-grove and when the wind blew they would pick ripe mangoes shaken off the trees. On the sly they would sometimes even fling a stone or two to help bring down the mangoes. If the guard saw them he would chase them off with his stick. Whenever Savitri found a nice ripe mango she would bring it and give it to him, to Vachaspati! 'Just for you,' she would say. Other girls would often tease her for this. Vachaspati would find such affection for himself on the part of Savitri quite intolerable. He had told her off a few times. But when Savitri had not seemed to get the message he had once given her a sound thrashing. When old man Trivedi had found out he had gone and complained to dear old Balmukunda. And when old man Balmukunda had in turn thrashed Vachaspati, his darling son had remained bedridden for a week. As was the honourable family custom Savitri had been withdrawn from school once she had passed standard eight.

The second kind of girls are these, Vachaspati would think: laden and hoist pell-mell on a rickshaw, going to pursue higher education. They are quite oblivious of where their sari is slipping off to or which way their palla is blowing, the end of the sari which should modestly fall in front. They are heedless of the fact that the hearts of all bystanders are fluttering at the sight of their breasts fastened in tight blouses. They are just giggling away to themselves. The very idea would thrill him that one day, having found the opportune moment and having plucked up his courage, he would go up to Miss Bannerji of his class and actually speak to her.

And the third kind of girl? They were those who had at the height of their youth spurned the love and comfort of their homes and had travelled ten thousand miles from America in search of the truth. They slept on the bare floors of free Hindu pilgrim-houses, they walked about barefoot on the ghats of Banaras at all hours of the day and night. From a boat on the river they photographed corpses burning on the Manikarnika, and by the light of the day they went walking in the narrow lane of the Vishwanath Temple with an arm around the waist of their male companions and with their bodies blithely brushing past all kinds of strange men.

Vachaspati liked this third kind of girl a lot. He wished he could join their group and show them the hidden kingdom of Banaras streets. He wished he could go on a boatride with them right from Asi to Manikarnika and recount to them the whole history of Banaras. He wished he could teach them Sanskrit, acquaint them with the great tradition of the Hindu religion and be their partner in their quest for the truth. Sometimes he would even try to persuade himself to abandon the wooden bed of his hostel and go and sleep on the cold floors of pilgrim-houses with those young women.

There were however two little hitches before he could do any of these. First, it was necessary for him to pass in the first division his M.Sc. examination if he were to keep his father from blowing his top and keep alive his chances of going to America. The second obstacle was more daunting still. Having passed his B.Sc. from the degree college in Chhapra, he could write English but he could hardly speak it. Now he began to practice speaking in English.

An opportunity for speaking to Miss Bannerji arose one day all of a sudden. After classes were over he observed Miss Bannerji walking to the library. Her usual girl-friends were not with her. Vachaspati promptly fell behind her. On the pretext of looking for books he kept spying on her from behind bookshelves. When Miss Bannerji had sat herself down at a desk with her book he made so bold as to go and sit opposite her at the same desk. Miss Bannerji read her book with total absorption and Vachaspati wondered furiously what to say to start a conversation. Just then he happened to look up at a wall which had a sign saying 'Silence Please.' This dampened such courage as he had been able to muster. After a few moments Miss Bannerji rummaged in her bag, looked up at Vachaspati and said, 'Excuse me, I forgot to bring my pen today. You wouldn't have one I could borrow, would you?'

One could have knocked Vachaspati down with a feather. He nearly broke out in a sweat. What he wanted to say was that he wished to lay down his life for her to say nothing of a pen, but no words escaped him. He mumbled something and began to search each of his pockets in turn for a pen. He too had forgotten to bring a pen. He got up all in a fluster saying, 'Just a moment.'

Tearing out in a rush he never heard Miss Bannerji say after him that it was all right, she had now found her pen. When he returned with a pen a little while later Miss Bannerji had already left. How he had cursed himself that day for not always keeping a pen on him. Through his two years of studying for the M. Sc., this remained the first and last encounter between Vachaspati and Miss Bannerji.

When he had begun prattling in English a little he decided that he would spend part of each Saturday afternoon at the Dashashwamedh Ghat. The idea was that this might lead to contact one day with the American maidens. He must have watched countless Saturday suns set on the Ghat, so much so that his friends began to say that this bugger Vachaspati had gone holy, for hadn't he started attending recitations of the *Ramayana* each Saturday at the Dashashwamedh?

One day there finally arrived that moment of truth for which Vachaspati had waited so patiently all along. Four or five American boys and girls had just returned from a boatride. Their leader and the boatmen were haggling over the fare. Vachaspati promptly decided that he would act as an arbiter and secure the goodwill of these foreigners. He ran up and began to talk to the boatmen. But strange are the ways of fate!

Just then there happened to pass by this class-mate Ram Daras Pande, who was in the habit of using the open *ghats* for, using his muscle-building clubs in, and on seeing Vachaspati he stopped. Pande bellowed to one of the boatmen: 'Hey Damri, what's the matter?'

Now who did not know Pande the Wrestler? Damri said, 'Sir, they are paying less than we'd agreed upon.'

Pande pronounced verdict instantly. He said to the foreign young man in English: '*Give money otherwise problem.*'

Vachaspati's ambition to introduce foreigners to Hindu culture remained buried in his heart until he arrived in America to do his Ph.D.

Not only did he pass his M.Sc. in the first division but he was ranked first in the whole university. One of his teachers who had himself been to America encouraged him strongly to go there to do his Ph. D. He also promised to try and get him a grant. Vachaspati mentioned this to his father. The news truly warmed the cockles of Pandit Balmukunda Sharma's heart but he did not let his son know. Instead, he said, 'If you are keen, you may go. It seems like a good opportunity. I have only one condition. I should want to marry you off before you go.'

Exactly a week after the marriage with Savitri, Pandit Balmukunda Sharma accompanied his son to Delhi and put him on a plane to America. The idea was that once he had reached and settled down in America arrangements would be made to send Savitri on. Little did dear father know that it would be another three years before Savitri reached America.

Barring the first few months of separation from his newly wedded wife, those three years were really the most glorious of Vachaspati's life. A new world lay open before him, and his heart was full of hope and excitement.

Accommodation had been booked for him in the men's hall. But neither the room nor the food there was to Vachaspati's liking at all. Just then he happened to meet Ramnath from Roorkee who was quite as unhappy with the whole set-up. The two got together and rented a small apartment. They bought a few cheap utensils.

Each evening they would cook an Indian meal and sit around and plan how to hook a girl. For many months they would study by day and plot by evening; what they finally decided to do was to call a lot of boys and girls to a meal. From among them they would pick out two girls. When these two girls had grown pretty friendly just the two of them would be called to dinner one night. This plan pleased the two friends no end and they slept the sleep of the just that night.

Whenever Vachaspati introduced himself to any girl he would say, 'The name is Vachaspati, but you may call me Vachis.'

Vachis and Ramnath threw a number of parties. Vachis initiated countless girls into Indian metaphysics, introduced them to a variety of vegetarian dishes and, so as to help relieve his homesickness and loneliness in a foreign land, encouraged them to spend the night with him. When he felt the need to be a little more independent after a few months he advised Ramnath to go and find a place of his own. Not that Ramnath's presence interfered in any way with any of his activities, but once he had left, the coast was entirely clear.

It gradually grew a little tiresome to have to cook meals, throw parties, talk all kinds of nonsense for hours and only then stalk the prey. One day however he had a real brainwave. Ramnath's room still lay vacant. What could possibly be better than if some dear little thing were to come and live with him and cook and clean for him and sleep with him as would his own wedded wife. What he wanted was to have no more than a clearly-defined relationship with this hypothetical maiden. He did not want this girl to hang like a millstone round his neck; after all Savitri in the village was patiently waiting for him and he would have to bring her over some time or the other. Soon enough, the day arrived when his plan was realized.

The post of a teaching assistant fell vacant in his department and he was appointed to it. His job was to grade the scripts for the professor and to counsel the students on their individual problems.

Now eighteen-year-old Cynthia Jones was a stunning beauty but not much physics got into her head. She got poor grades in her first two semesters. Vachis not only suggested but fairly-well insisted that with just a little bit of help she could really come up in the class.

112

'But everybody in the department is ever so busy. Who would have the time to help me out? And even if I could persuade someone to give me private lessons I could never afford it. As it is I can hardly make ends meet.'

Vachis gave Cynthia's problem his most serious consideration. Then he said, 'Look, why don't you come here this time tomorrow. By then I should have worked out something or the other.'

When Cynthia turned up the following day Vachis had thought up a solution to the problem. 'I did ask around. Either they don't have the time—at any rate those who might be suitable for you. Or, if one or two are suitable, they want too much money.'

Cynthia's face fell.

'But that's no reason to be depressed.' After a little silence Vachis added most solemnly, 'My father is a renowned scholar of Sanskrit. His whole life has been spent teaching students—especially students who did not have the money for their studies. I have learnt a lot at the feet of my father—and what I have learnt above everything else is this, that one should entirely dedicate one's life to one's students.'

Then he added, pausing now and then, 'You know how the work for my Ph. D. leaves me quite done in. On top of that I have now got this teaching to do. In this department, one doesn't have a moment to call one's soul one's own. But, having thought about it, I have decided that I shall teach you privately two or three times a week—if that's all right by you.'

Cynthia couldn't believe her ears. She said, 'Will you, really!' and got up and in her excitement gave Vachis a good hug. 'Yes, it's all right by me, Vachis, of course it is. Thank you! Do you know, you are a really kind man?'

'It is but my duty. Let us now work out the details. When, which days and where.'

Cynthia accepted all that Vachis proposed. She would come to Vachis's every Wednesday and Friday at seven in the evening, he would teach her for an hour or so, and maybe she would then have dinner with him. On her part, she wanted to do something to repay all this kindness. Could she perhaps clean and wash up for him? No, no, that wouldn't be necessary. But she really would love to. All right then, if it pleased her he had no objection.

The guru-disciple relationship between Vachis and Cynthia did not remain so for long. One Friday when Cynthia arrived at Vachis's she found him looking quite disconsolate. He said, 'I don't really feel like teaching today.'

This was said in such a tone that Cynthia believed something really must be the matter. She asked, 'What is it, Vachis?'

'I am very sad today.'

'Can I do something to help?'

'No.'

'If you'd rather be alone I'd go.'

'No, Cynthia, come and sit down. I'll feel better with you around.'

'But then tell me what it is.'

'What can I tell you, Cynthia? A tempest of thoughts is brewing in my mind. I don't know what it is.'

'Come, let me rub your forehead. That should make you feel better.'

Cynthia was at that moment both an eighteen-year-old girl and a mother to baby Vachis. She stood behind his chair and began gently massaging his forehead. Vachis shut his eyes. After a little while he said, 'That feels very nice. But you must be getting tired.'

'No, not at all. I have hardly begun.'

'Well, if you aren't tired already you will soon tire standing like that. I'll tell you what. Why don't you sit down at one end of the sofa, and I'll lie down and put my head in your lap. Wouldn't that be more comfortable?'

Vachis lay down with his head in Cynthia's lap and she began stroking his head and his hair. Vachis liked this very much, and especially the touch of Cynthia's full breasts which were tickling his head and nape. After a few moments he raised his arms and softly drew Cynthia's face to his own and kissed her on the lips.

A week after this Cynthia moved into the room left vacant by Ramnath. Vachaspati on his part never gave any indication that there was any permanence or emotional complication in his relationship with Cynthia. But even without any such commitment Cynthia had given her body and her soul to her dear Vachis. She even dreamt of a future together.

The dream world of Cynthia and the intellectual and physical fulfillment enjoyed by Vachis both came to an end three years later when news arrived from the village that Pandit Balmukunda Sharma had suffered a sudden heart attack and had passed away.

When Vachaspati broke this news to Cynthia she began to cry.

'If you go now you will never come back!'

This wasn't quite true. Vachaspati knew that he would of course return but he knew too that Savitri would come with him. He had never mentioned Savitri to Cynthia. He said, 'Of course I'll come back . . . '

Cynthia clung to him. This did not thrill Vachis in the same way as when he had first taken her in his arms while she had rubbed his forehead. He felt as if some she-serpent had coiled herself round his body. He unwound her body from his as if peeling off the skin of an orange. Then he said, 'This is a very serious matter. When I return we shan't be able to live together . . . '

Cynthia began to cry all over again. When her tears let her speak she asked, 'But why? Why do you say so?'

Vachaspati couldn't at once think what to say. After thinking it over for a while he resumed, 'I am the eldest son in my family. According to custom I must marry immediately once my father is dead. I shall be married off at home.'

Cynthia gazed at him with her large eyes unblinkingly, as if she couldn't believe him.

'And what will happen to me then? If you must marry why can't you take me with you? Then you could marry me.'

'No, that will not be possible. In this I shall have to go by the wishes of my widowed mother.'

Cynthia kept crying and Vachaspati kept trying to console her. Before he left he drove her, bag and baggage, to her sister's house.

Vachaspati reached Chhapra with a heavy heart. Father had already been cremated. He stayed on at home for some days and then returned to America with Savitri and began the life of a Hindu householder. One year after his return Munni was born. After Munni came two little gems of sons. When he had finished his Ph.D. he got a job at the same university.

*

Having finished seasoning the vegetable dish of mustard leaf Savitri lowered the flame, put a lid on the pan and left it to simmer, and came and sat down by her husband.

'What are you thinking of?'

'Oh! What time is it?'

'Seven o'clock.'

'And Munni isn't home yet?'

'But today's Saturday, isn't it? She goes on Saturdays to babysit for the Smiths. She'll be back only at eight.'

'I don't like all this one bit.'

'What?'

'That Munni should keep away from home till so late.'

'But she is working, isn't she. She earns two dollars an hour. And then Mr Smith himself drives her back.'

'How old is Mr Smith?'

'Why do you ask? He'd be thirty, maybe thirty-two.'

'I don't want my daughter to go out and work. What does she lack at home?'

'Just listen to you talk! She was born in America, she was brought up here, she is an all-American girl. All other girls her age work.'

'Savitri, you don't understand. Munni is all but grown up now. Sometimes I really worry about her.'

'And hadn't I once grown up?'

'But that was different.'

'And how?'

'You were born and brought up in your own culture. There is a world of a difference between values there and values here.'

'But how?'

'How should I explain? Over there, women are respected. There is a decorum in the matter of man-woman relationships which is customary and which no one can even think of violating. Ours is an ancient civilization and our social conduct derives from that civilization. In that society our daughters are safe and so are our daughters-in-law. But the West is—how shall I put it—a jungle!'

Savitri was secretly pleased that even after so many years her husband remained uncorrupted by the West. But she said, 'You worry about nothing. If she has imbibed even some of the values of her parents our Munni will be well able to look after herself. And she has learnt a few things here as well, hasn't she? I trust her completely.'

'So do I. But I don't trust wolves on the prowl.'

'But what can you do? You can't lock her up, can you!'

Dr Vachaspati Sharma suddenly flew into a rage. With a flick of the button he switched the TV off. He picked up his flabby self from the sofa and stood up erect.

'You have no notion what I can do!' And then without waiting for a reply he added, 'No, you haven't the faintest idea. I can marry her off instantly. Not with some American layabout stud but with a cultured Indian young man.'

He began pacing up and down the room in great agitation.

'Tomorrow morning, I will write to Uncle in Chhapra about this.'

Dr Vachaspati Sharma sank into the sofa. He switched the TV on again and was again lost in it.

Savitri smiled to see her husband in a rage, and returned to the kitchen. She fondly recalled the day he had thrashed her in the mango grove. She was confirmed in her conviction that he still had the moral rectitude and vigour left to protect her and their children.

She bowed her head in reverence to her husband and to his forebears.

Translated from the Hindi by Harish Trivedi

H. S. Venkateshamurthy

Electric Lights Come to Puttalli*

Children wake up run a rope round the pulley
of the jasmine well and water laughs
birds preen their wings something flashes
in the field and urchins play *cinni dandu***
near the river

carts silently descend in the distance
cart behind cart behind cart behind cart

as the sun climbs the sky shadows lean
water warms in the river the rays pour
all over bald heads and down down down
come people in carts magical people
wearing blue

bringing poles the whole length of the carts
stretching before and behind
weird calculations at the edge of the brain
scratching at wonder a fear of deep things
at the fingertips

climbing them with eyes speaking silent meanings
the people wearing blue bring down the poles

---

* Puttalli: little village.
**Cinni dandu: a game played with a short whittled piece (*cinni*) and a longer stick
 (*dandu*).

balance them from street to street multiplying
numbers and leaving bootprints without a toe
snake-hood patterns in the dirt

uncoiling a coil of copper digging pits
planting poles pouring salt pouring water
burying a meaning in a language no one knows there
leaving not a street alley corner or turning
they spread a net of wire

grow long in shadow as the day declines
becoming night with anxiety's nets of wire below
crowds gather as at a fair mouths gaping
standing rooted like rows of poles like the rows
of electric poles

even as they look on the blue ones suddenly
laugh climb up and up on the poles the blue people
become specks and melt away in the blue

Translated from the Kannada by A. K. Ramanujan

Along the Railroad Track

In our childhood days,
On the way to our country place
We could see the paddy fields stretching for miles
Patterned with red spinach.
A vast expanse of green,
Lush with crops, and more crops.
The eternal wag-tailed swallow
Perched on the telegraph wires
The farmer, in the drizzling rain
Palm-leaf hat upon his head
And many more wonders
Waiting
Along the railroad track.

Today, many years later
Even more sinister wonders
Wait along the track,
These days a new addition—
A harvest of violent clashes
Nights,
Along the slippery ridges of the paddy fields
Where the field-snake lies relaxed among the dewdrops
Hearing the familiar footsteps of the farmer,
Slips away into the field.
There,
Near the railway station of Belanagar or of Pandua
Beside the iron rails

The headless corpse of a young boy lies.
And, in future years, grimmer wonders
Await us.
Rumour has it—
A strange new red spinach pattern will be woven
With the blood of a young farmboy.

Translated from the Bengali by Paramita Banerjee and Arlene Zide

A Ten Day Fast

10 January

Today I said to Bannu, 'Look here, Bannu, these days nothing works—the parliament, the judges, the bureaucracy, nothing. These days all major demands are gained only through threats of fasts and self-immolation. Our democracy is twenty years old. It's now so fine-tuned that the threat of just one man going hungry or killing himself can decide the fate of millions of people. Now's the time you went on an indefinite fast—for that woman.'

Bannu remained silent. For sixteen years he has been after Radhika Babu's wife, Savitri. Once he even got badly roughed up when he tried to drag her away. Bannu can't get her to leave her husband and come live with him because Savitri hates even the sight of his face.

Finally, after some deep thought, Bannu said, 'But can one go on a fast in such a matter?'

'These days you can fast for anything,' I replied. 'Just recently Baba Sanakidas went on a fast and got a new law passed: it requires people to grow long hair but never shampoo. Now everyone has a stinking head. Compared to that, your demand is a mere trifle—you only want that woman.'

'What're you talking about!' Surendra, who had been listening to us, spoke up. 'Go on a fast to grab someone else's wife? You should be ashamed of yourself. We'll be the laughing-stock of the neighbourhood.'

'Look,' I tried to explain, 'even great sadhus and saints don't feel any shame in going on fasts, so what's the big fuss about us common folks? As for people laughing at us, they've already laughed so much at the Cow Protection Movement they can't laugh any more. Even if they were to try they'd only cry out in pain. In fact, for the next ten years no one dares to laugh lest he kill himself.'

'But will I succeed?' Bannu asked.

'That depends on how you set up the "issue". If the "issue" is set up well you'll get your woman.' I then continued, 'Let's go to an expert and get his advice. Baba Sanakidas is your man. He has quite a thing going these days. Right now he has four men fasting under his directions.'

We went to Baba Sanakidas. He listened to us, then said, 'Fine. I can take your case. Just do as I tell you.' Then, turning to Bannu, he asked, 'Can you threaten to set fire to yourself?'

Bannu was shaking with fear. He whimpered, 'I'm scared.'

'You won't have to burn yourself. Just threaten that you might.'

'I can't even think of it,' Bannu cried. 'It scares me to death.'

'In that case,' Baba said, 'you should go on a fast. As for setting up the "issue", leave it to me. I'll take care of it.'

Bannu was still very nervous. 'I won't have to die, will I?' he asked.

Baba replied, 'Smart people don't die. They keep one eye on their medical chart, the other on the mediator. But don't you worry, we won't let you die. We'll also get you the woman.'

11 January

Bannu has settled down in a tent for his 'fast-unto-death.' Incense sticks burn near him, and a group is lustily singing Mahatma Gandhi's favourite song, *'Sab Ko Sammati De Bhagwan.'** The atmosphere is very sacral, even on this first day. There is no doubt that Baba Sanakidas is a master of his art. The 'Declaration of Principles' that he wrote and distributed on Bannu's behalf is simply brilliant. In it Bannu says: 'My soul is calling out to me, "I'm as yet only one-half. My other half is in Savitri." My soul says, "Bring the two halves together and make them one. Or else set me

---

* May God grant peace to everyone.

123

free from this body." I'm going on this fast to bring the two halves of my soul together. My demand is that Savitri should be given to me. If I don't get her I'll fast unto death to let my half of the soul be rid of this transient body. I fear nothing, for I stand for truth. May Truth be victorious!'

Savitri came into the tent, boiling with rage. She said to Baba Sanakidas, 'The bastard is fasting to get me, isn't he?'

'Devi,' the Baba gently replied, 'you shouldn't abuse him. His fast is pure. He may have been a bastard earlier, but he isn't one any more. He's now on a fast-unto-death.'

'But he should've asked me first,' Savitri retorted. 'I spit on him.'

In his calmest voice the Baba said, 'Devi, you're merely the "issue", and no one asks the "issue" in such matters. Did the Cow Protection Movement people ask the cow before they launched their campaign? You should go home, devi. If you ask my advice, neither you nor your husband should come here any more. In a day or two, when the public opinion is fully formed, some people may not stand for your nasty comments.'

Savitri went away muttering under her breath.

Bannu turned gloomy. The Baba tried to console him: 'Don't worry. Victory will be yours. In the end, Truth always comes out victorious.'

13 January

It seems Bannu has little tolerance for hunger. Today is only the third day, but he's started to moan and groan.

He asked me, 'Has Jayaprakash Narayan come yet?'

'He comes only on the fifth day,' I explained, 'or on the sixth. That's his principle. We have, of course, informed him.'

A few minutes later Bannu asked, 'What did Vinobha say?'

'He made some comments on the relative importance of the means and the ends,' Baba Sanakidas replied. 'But with a little word-twisting we can use his remarks to support our position.'

Bannu closed his eyes. He said, 'Brother, get Jayaprakash Babu here soon.'

Today some journalists came to see us. They asked all sorts of questions. 'What caused him to fast?' 'Is it a public cause?'

'One doesn't ask about the cause at this stage,' the Baba told them. 'The problem now is how to save Bannu's life. When someone goes on a fast he makes such a sacrifice that no matter what the cause it becomes pure.'

'There will be some public benefit too,' I added. 'Many of us secretly wish to snatch other men's wives, but don't know what to do. If this fast succeeds, it will show the public the right path to follow.'

14 January

Bannu has become quite weak. He has been threatening to end the fast. That would be a disaster. Baba Sanakidas had to spend a lot of time convincing him.

Today the Baba did another amazing thing. He had a statement by some Swami Rasananddas published in the papers. The Swami has declared: 'I have performed many ascetic acts. Those acts have given me the power to see both the past and the future. I have discovered that Bannu was a sage in his previous life, and that Savitri was his wife. In that life, Bannu's name was Rishi Vanamanus. Now, after three thousand years, he has again taken the body of a man. He and Savitri had sacred marital ties in all their previous births. It's a terrible sin that a sage's wife should now live in the house of an ordinary man like Radhika Prasad. I plead to all Dharma-loving people: they shouldn't let this sinful state continue any further.'

The statement has had good effect. Some people came to our camp, shouting, 'Victory to Dharma!' Another large group went to Radhika Babu's house and shouted: 'Radhika Prasad is a sinner!' 'May the sinner soon perish!' 'Victory to Dharma!'

The Swami also arranged to have prayers said in several temples for the protection of Bannu's life.

15 January

Last night someone threw stones into Radhika Babu's house. Public opinion has crystallized. These are some of the remarks our 'spies' heard around the city: 'Poor Bannu! He's been without food for five days!' 'I really admire his determination.' 'But that cruel woman hasn't softened at all.' 'Look at her husband, what a shameless man!' 'I hear Bannu was a sage in his previous birth.' 'Why, didn't you read Swami Rasananddas's statement?' 'They say it's a great sin to keep a sage's wife as your own.'

Today eleven virtuous, married women came and performed a ritual to honour Bannu. Bannu was delighted. Whenever he sees a virtuous, married woman his heart leaps with joy.

The newspapers are full of the news of the fast.

Today we sent a small crowd to the Prime Minister's house to appeal to him to interfere in the matter and save Bannu's life. The PM refused to meet with them. (We'll see about that.)

Jayaprakash Narayan arrived this evening. He was rather severe. 'How many lives must I save?' he asked, crossly. 'Is that my profession now? Every other day someone starts a fast, then shouts "Save me". If you want your life saved, why not eat something? You don't need a mediator to save your life. Such nonsense! Now they're using the virtuous tool of a fast to grab another man's wife!'

We explained to him: 'This is a different kind of "issue". It's Bannu's soul that has cried out.'

Jayaprakash Narayan calmed down; he said, 'If it's a cry of his soul then I'll willingly lend a hand.'

'The voices of millions of virtuous people have also joined,' I added.

Jayaprakash Babu agreed to mediate. He'll first meet with Savitri and her husband, then go to see the PM.

All the while, Bannu gazed at Jayaprakash Babu with abject, grateful eyes.

Later we told him: 'You bastard, don't look so pathetic. If one of the leaders catches on to you he'd immediately offer you a glass of orange juice. Don't you see so many of them are hanging around your tent, with shoulderbags full of oranges?'

16 January

Jayaprakash Babu has failed in his 'mission.' No one is willing to agree. The PM said, 'We sympathize with Bannu, but there's nothing we can do. Get him to break his fast first, then we'll have talks to find a solution.'

We were disappointed.

But not Baba Sanakidas. He said, 'At first everyone rejects the demand. That's the convention. Now we must enhance our struggle. We should put in the papers that there was much "acetone" in Bannu's urine today, that his deteriorating condition is causing great anxiety. Other statements should also appear demanding that Bannu's life must be saved at any cost. Why's the government not doing anything? It should immediately take steps to save Bannu's priceless life.'

The Baba is simply amazing. Who knows what schemes are tucked away inside his head!

He continued, 'The time has come to introduce the question of caste in our campaign. Bannu is a Brahmin, Radhika Prasad is a Kayastha. Some people should work on the Brahmins, others on the Kayasthas. I understand the head of the Brahmin Sabha plans to run in the next general elections. Explain to him that this may be his big chance to get all the Brahmin votes.'

Today a request came from Radhika Babu; he wanted Bannu to let Savitri tie a *rakhi* on his wrist and thus make him her 'brother'.

We rejected the offer.

17 January

The headlines today were: 'Save Bannu's life.' 'Bannu's condition causes anxiety.' 'Prayers said in temples to save Bannu's life.'

In one paper we had the following ad put in:

Millions of Virtuous People Demand

Bannu's Life Must Be Saved

Horrible Consequences If Bannu Dies

The President of the Brahmin Sabha has issued a statement. He sees the situation as a challenge to the honour of all Brahmins. He threatens to take 'direct action'.

We have hired four local bullies. Tonight they'll throw stones into Kayastha homes; afterwards, they'll go to the Brahmin neighbourhood and do the same there. Bannu had to pay them in advance.

The Baba thinks that by tomorrow or the day after we should get the authorities to impose a curfew. Or at least make them declare into effect 'Section 144' of the Penal Code. The Baba says that will make our 'case' stronger.

18 January

Last night stones were thrown into Brahmin and Kayastha homes.

In the morning there was a pitched battle between several groups of the two castes, who freely threw stones at each other.

'Section 144' of the Penal Code has now been imposed on the city, restricting public assembly.

The city is tense.

A delegation of our representatives met with the Prime Minister. He told them, 'There are legal problems here. This may require some changes in the Marriage Law.'

'Then you should make the changes. Or issue an ordinance,' we replied. 'For if Bannu dies the entire country will go up in flames.'

He said, 'First get him to end the fast.'

'No, the government should first accept the principle of his demand and set up a committee,' we countered. 'That committee could then find some way for this man to get his woman.'

The government is still watching the situation carefully. Bannu will have to suffer some more. The matter is at a standstill; the talks are at a 'deadlock'.

Small skirmishes continue.

Last night we had some stones thrown at the police station. That had satisfactory results.

The slogan, 'Save the Life', is now heard much louder.

19 January

Bannu has become extremely weak. He's scared he might die. He raves that we've let him walk into a trap. We're worried: if he issues a statement we'd all be exposed.

We must do something soon. We have warned Bannu that if

he were to break his fast now when nothing's been gained, the public will lynch him.

Our delegation is to see the PM again.

20 January

'Deadlock!' the headlines screamed.

Only one bus could be burned today. Bannu is in very bad shape.

We issued a statement on his behalf: 'I may die but I shall not retreat.'

The government too seems rather worried.

Today the All India Sadhu Sabha endorsed our demand.

The Brahmin Society has issued an ultimatum: 'If the demand's not met ten Brahmins will immolate themselves.'

Savitri tried to commit suicide but was saved.

There is a constant line of people outside who want to have Bannu's *darshan*.

A telegram has been sent to the Secretary General of the UN.

Prayer meetings are being held all over the country.

Dr Ram Manohar Lohia, the Socialist leader, has issued a statement: 'So long as the present government remains in power no just demand of the people can be expected to be met. We suggest that instead of going after Savitri, Bannu ought to run away with the government itself.'

21 January

The government has accepted Bannu's demand in principle.

A committee has been set up to resolve procedural problems.

Amidst loud singing of bhajans and prayers, Baba Sanakidas offered a glass of orange juice to Bannu. The Baba declared, 'In a democracy, public opinion has to be respected. This issue involved the sentiments of millions of people. It's good that it was resolved peacefully. Otherwise a violent revolution could have occurred.'

The man from the Brahmin Sabha has made a deal with Bannu; Bannu will campaign on his behalf in the next general elections. He has given Bannu plenty of money. Bannu's price has gone up.

To the hundreds of men and women who are coming to touch his feet in adoration, Bannu says, 'What happened was God's wish; I was merely His medium.'

People are shouting: 'Victory to Truth.' 'Victory to Dharma.'

Translated from the Hindi by C. M. Naim

Street Dog

It happened years ago—
When you and I went our separate ways
With no regrets
Only—there's just one thing I never understood.

You and I, when we said farewell
Our house on sale,
The empty pots and pans
Scattered in the courtyard
            Maybe watching us
The others upside down
            Maybe hiding their faces.

A withered vine above the door
Maybe trying to say something to us, me and you
            Or complaining to the water tap.

None of this, or things like this
Ever come to mind these days
Only—one thing keeps coming back.

How a street dog—
Strayed into our empty room
Sniffing each and every corner
And the door closed on him from outside.
Then three days later—
When the deal was closed

And we traded keys for cash
Handed over the locks, and one by one
Showed the new owner all the rooms
In one of them was that dog's corpse.

I never heard his bark
              Just smelled his stench
And suddenly, from several things
It's that very stench I smell now too.

Translated from the Punjabi by Arlene Zide and the poet

A Strange Man

A strange man. At his every step,
the enmity of thorns. When he tries to speak,
the sounds turn to rainbows. He stands
amazed, like a lover who knows
he has no right to burn.

His friends know they must save him
from himself. They probe and probe
till a wound wells up, endless, satisfying
as a tame bird's death. Still, he says,
spirits dance on the mountain at night.

Says it, and watches as his blood
becomes the afternoon's river
to the stars. Now the clouds
will enter the water to make the evening bright.
His heart is an unopened flower, skilled in pain.

Circles of women close in and ripple
at him, their bodies shining
as brass pitchers. Strange man, they say.
He sees only the magnolias in the western sky.
The spear of beauty has blinded both his eyes.

The day he dies into that darkness,
the mice come, the foxes. The remnants
of his flesh decay into the earth.
Only the bones open white into lotuses
in a silence charged with the song of the bees.

Translated from the Bengali by Chitra Divakaruni

Shelter[*]

Bagiradi Patti (Grandmother Bagiradi) was going through
Manimedai Junction. As soon as the clock struck seven she began
to run. Her body jiggled, her head bobbed, as she dashed four feet,
walked two. The little porter boy followed behind, running. It was
quite a spectacle. There were not many people around, though, to
savour the scene. Manimedai had not yet taken on its usual
appearance of hustle and bustle. It had just opened its eyes, but it
still lazed in bed wiggling its feet.

Patti was running now.

A porter, who had tied his *dhoti*[**] up around his neck, rested
his hands on his knees by the Lala Sweet Shop and grinned through
his tobacco-stained teeth. The sweeper woman sweeping the street
also enjoyed the sight. Only a couple of people who were heading
for the market did not pay any attention.

At the turning there was a line of horse carts. A cartman who
had curled up with his head in the cab of the coach looked up. 'Run
fast, lady, the bus has started to move,' he said, urging her on,
mischievously.

Patti didn't pay any attention to where the voice came from;
as if obeying a heavenly voice, she tried running faster. But she
could run no faster than before. 'Uh, oh,' she said, her head and
ample body shaking.

As soon as she passed the turning she could see the bus
standing in the distance. She slowed down and proceeded at a

[*] The translators wish to thank Raja Balasundararaman.
[**] Dhoti: a loose garment wrapped around the lower body.

rather more leisurely pace. She couldn't walk anymore. Her breath heaved in and out. Sweat poured off her. Her mouth hung open.

That bus standing there, where is it going? Who knows? It was satisfying enough just to see a bus standing.

She had not started off thinking that a bus left for Tirukkanangudi at seven o'clock. She didn't know when the bus was leaving. She had just headed off on her own. As soon as the clock had started to chime an urgency overcame her and sent her on her way. Why she was running, she didn't know.

The bus that was standing began to move. Patti made an effort to run again.

'Hey, lady, where do you need to go?'

'I've got to go to Tirukkanangudi, *appa*.'

'This bus goes to Tirunelveli. Take it easy. Why are you running for nothing?'

Patti just stood there.

Before the coolie's wage was settled there was a long drawn out argument. The driver, the conductor, and the bus-stand agent mediated the peace. Thinking 'let it go,' Patti hurled another half paisa at him. She was too embarrassed to be found standing in the middle of the street, complaining.

'When is the bus to Tirukkanangudi, *appa*?' she asked.

'Only at a quarter past eight,' replied the driver.

Patti bought herself a ticket.

'Why are you standing in the middle of the street? Have a seat on the pyol* over there.'

Patti moved her belongings one by one over to the pyol.

A basket full of greens from Chenpakaraman Puthur. She had covered the top with a wet cloth and tied it up. A large box, closed and locked. A bundle of clothes; two saris entwined like coupling snakes twisted and one looking at the other. Faded white. A vegetable knife. Brand new. The instrument's handle was bright yellow. The blade of the knife was wrapped in an old cloth, for the benefit of fellow travellers.

If she put all four things on the pyol, Patti would have to remain standing. She tucked the box and the basket of greens

---

* Pyol: a narrow, bench-like structure attached to the front of a building.

underneath her legs. Then she sat down on the pyol, arranging the vegetable knife and bundle of clothes on either side of her, fondly hugging them to herself with both hands.

Patti sat there in state. Anyone standing in the station would have been struck by her.

Her face was round like a young palmyra fruit. Her protruding, bent forehead made her eyes sink into pits. A bell pepper nose. Sagging cheeks hung down drawing two deep lines on either side of her nose. Fine hairs on the edges of her ears. Black lips. Small, silver-rimmed glasses on her nose. Because the ear stems were broken, she had tied a string to her glasses and wrapped it all the way around her head. Fold after fold of plump flesh hung pleasantly from her arms and belly.

The early morning rays chased away the shadows.

Her stomach churned as each bus started off. She feared that her bus would leave without picking her up. They may go off saying, 'Forget the old bag.' Patti would enquire first with one person, skip one (so the first one would not hear) and then ask another.

When she suddenly turned around, she noticed a foreign woman standing 'tip top' right next to her. Oh no!

Patti watched her. The woman snatched her glasses from her nose, held them straight in front of her face and looked up through them at the sky. The next second, she licked the glasses front and back, unfurled her handkerchief and began wiping them.

Patti's stomach was turning. What a creature! Her face contorted in disgust. *Chee*, the wretch!

She again raised her head to the woman's face. A beautiful face. Fair isn't the word—shining white. Curly, curly hair. So thick, a finger would get stuck in it. As soon as she saw the beauty of that hair, Patti was overcome with the desire to plait her hair with fragrant *thalam* flowers. What an ass! She's gone and cut her gorgeous hair like a horse's tail. How could she have the heart to do that?

Hm, these are upside-down times.

*

If at six o'clock in the morning you saw her daughter Yechumi, bathed with turmeric, a wet towel wrapped around her hair and sitting in front of the holy basil plant, your hands would just come together by themselves. Patti was disturbed, not being able to tear her eyes away, and asked herself, would a mother cast the evil eye on her own child?

She had invited them, again and again, insistently. She wrote letter after letter. Fine. Deciding that she would herself go visit them for a while, Patti had started off to Delhi when she got someone to travel with her. She had had enough—that lovely little visit!

Her daughter's husband and the children had come to the station. Cigarette dangling from his lips, the husband had raised his left hand in welcome to his mother-in-law. Fourteen-year-old Sachu, wearing a gown with a muffler wrapped around her neck, saw Patti and grinned.

Patti had gone to Delhi with great expectations. Her son-in-law was a train station canteen manager. He even said that he might take her on a pilgrimage to Varanasi. She wouldn't have to spend a penny. One needs good fortune to get a glimpse of the god. Is that something easy to come by?

Even so, Patti left for home within two weeks.

'I don't want to go to Varanasi, I don't want to put an end to my karma. Get someone good to escort me and send me home.'

'What, don't you like Delhi city life?' asked the son-in-law.

Of course, she didn't like it. Could she tell him she didn't like it? It would be like a slap in the face. 'Don't you like Delhi?' Look at the question! What can Delhi do? Can it wear sacred ash on its forehead in perfect lines, and stand up in front of me, donning a *dhoti* Brahmin-style? If people's sense of propriety has gone bad, what can a town do?

Whom to blame? There was no fault in the birth, no fault in the upbringing nor in teaching them custom and conduct. Hadn't she woken up early every morning, and dashed about seeing to all the chores in the house? These days it is well past eight before husbands and wives, who lie together in the main hall, roll out of bed and wake up yawning, 'Ah, oooh . . .' They've even forgotten the practice of bundling up and putting away their bedding. From the youngest to the oldest member of the family, as soon as they get up they make straight for the kitchen, and only then open their eyes. Hot coffee, strong coffee . . . hot coffee, strong coffee . . . Of course, they shouldn't have to do anything like brush their teeth! Are they crazy, or what, to brush their teeth?!!

'Hey, how many times have I told you not to bite your nails?' Patti would say.

'Shut up!'

A child no bigger than a small rice measure. Named Romeo! That was the way he spoke. Whatever anyone said, 'Shut up' was the response. Shut up, or things like that.

'Hey, Lilly, go out wearing this half-sari. You'll be fourteen this coming August.'

'Go away, Patti, you don't know anything. Everyone here would laugh at me. They'd make fun of me and say, "*Ammami*," the Matron has come to town.'

Of course they'll laugh at you. Only if you roam around like a Marathi servant woman will they take you as one of their own, you fat potful of smartness, you.

Why talk about children? Everything depends on the mother. If the mother leaps eight feet, the children will leap sixteen.

She couldn't bear to look at Yechumi now wearing that jumper and sari. *Chee, chee!*

One early morning Patti was sitting outside on the pyol. A street hawker set his basket down on it.

'What have you got there?'

He said something or other in an unintelligible language. Patti waved her hand. He lifted the cloth from the basket and showed her. Chicken eggs!

Patti just covered her eyes and came inside. One day after that her daughter quietly told her. They're the only thing her husband will have for breakfast; he says he can't exist without them, he says they're the only things suitable for the cold weather.

Oh fine. Ambasamudram Vishvanatha Kanapatikal's first-born son cannot make do without chicken eggs. Oh, what a world!

Shouldn't say anything. We can't think badly of our children. Shouldn't talk ill of them. Yet, she'd never seen nor heard anything like this.

*

The stench of smoke was irritating her nose. She turned around. The foreign lady was smoking. Now this, to add to her ladyship's elegance?

Even so, wouldn't a woman feel ashamed to smoke beedis among all these men, standing right in their midst? What barbarous country's habit is this?

After a little while, Patti turned toward the woman. She had been standing looking in the opposite direction, but now she had turned and was facing Patti. Only then did Patti notice that the lady was pregnant, full term. Oh, the poor thing!

Why has she chosen this time to travel? Maybe something is urgent. What if? Would a woman start out on a trip in such a condition? She's just a girl. She wouldn't know better. She must have headed out on her own. If there were any elders in the house they would never have let her past the doorstep. She's probably an orphan like me.

Couldn't she have brought along a female companion? There must be a husband, right? Even if there isn't a husband, aren't there any children? There must definitely be a sister, a sister-in-law, a mother-in-law, somebody.

There could be a thousand reasons, but she should not have set off at this bad time. In her state, one day is not like the next. If the baby inside decides to see the world, who can stop it? If she goes into labour on the bus it'll be such an embarrassment. What a fool!

Hmm, is this something she doesn't know? After all, these are educated people! It's only folks like us who worry, whose hearts beat fast.

Patti gave the foreign woman another close look.

The sun was shining on the place where the woman was standing. Sweat was pouring off her neck. Her face had turned as red as vermilion. She dabbed her face frequently with her handkerchief, and shifted from one leg to the other.

Patti saw the swelling of the green veins in her legs and unconsciously rapped her knuckles on her forehead.

Without blinking, Patti stared at the woman's face. A very thin body, as if it had no blood whatsoever. This type of case will have a great deal of difficulty delivering a baby. This is the kind of woman who suffers unbearable labour pains. Her stomach had already sunk low. The veins on her throat stood out, throbbing. There were hollows in her collarbone.

Even so, just let her be. Just let her give birth and become two people without pain, in good health. Oh God! Separate the mother from the child, safely, that is enough. After that, it's up to the human beings.

Whatever was Patti thinking? She slipped down from the pyol, lifted the vegetable knife and the bundle of clothes and laid them on the ground.

'Hey,' she called out to the foreign woman.

The woman looked at Patti thinking that she was calling someone else.

'Hey, yes you. I've been watching you for some time. You've been standing there like a potted plant, eh! Don't you realize that there's a life hanging in your stomach? Look here! Be a nice girl and come have a seat right here,' said Patti in Tamil, showing her the pyol with her hands.

Patti moved over to a corner on the pyol. The woman bumped into Patti as she sat down next to her.

Translated from the Tamil by
J. Bernard Bate and A. K. Ramanujan

Wayside Station

There was the fragrance of some flowers
And there were flowers.
Children were selling in leaf-bags
Small wild plums,
An old woman in a dark blue torn sari
Was running panting and panicking
To catch the train about to depart.

At the back there was a wide open sky
Where fields began.

There was a crowd
And not a single familiar face.
But they were people who were quite familiar.

A yellow turban on his head
A middle-aged man squatted on the ground
With wife, a few children,
Waiting for some other train.

Translated from the Hindi by Harish Trivedi

The Battle of Man and Fish

We are putting into the sea
The fish that have been living in sweet water
Because sweet water fish sell well
Because we catch fish from the sea
Because our monster trawlers
Will not go into rivers.

We catch fish so that we may
Tin them and market them
Tinned fish are an emblem of our democracy
Available to all in place of fresh fish.

We are mastering science
To be able to put fish into tins
We are devising new ways not to let fish live in sweet water
But our scientific statistics tell us
That the fish put into the sea
Has an indomitable urge to return to sweet water.

We are fattening the breed of fish
So it may taste better and cost more.

The fish is fattening and yearns
Mightily to return to sweet water.

Science leads us to the conclusion
That having put the fish into the sea
We must then quickly kill it
So that it may not return to the river.

Translated from the Hindi by Harish Trivedi

The Handicapped Caught in a Camera

We shall appear on television
We the able and the strong
We shall bring a poor man
Into a closed room

We shall ask him, So are you a handicapped person?
But why are you a handicapped person?
Your handicap must give you pain
Now does it?
(Camera, come in, a big close up)
Yes, so tell us about your pain, then
What is this pain, quickly?

He wouldn't be able to tell.

Now think
Just tell us
How does it feel to be a handicapped person?
How
I mean how does it feel

(We shall ourselves helpfully gesture and hint;
Does it feel so?)
Now think
Tell us
Just concentrate
(We can't lose this opportunity!)

You know how to make the programme interesting
We shall ask and ask and reduce him to tears
Do you also wait for him to start crying?
Do you?
(This question will not be asked.)

Then we shall show on the screen
A blow up of a blinded eye
A big big blow up
And on his lips a twitch
(We hope you'll take it for the pain of the handicapped.)

One more attempt
Viewers
Please stay with us
Keep watching.
We must get both to start crying at once
You and him
Both.

(Camera
Cut
It didn't work
Never mind
Time on the screen is precious.)
Now we shall smile.

You were watching a socially purposeful programme
(Which all but came off)
Thank you.

Translated from the Hindi by Harish Trivedi

Raghuvir Sahay

Fear

This woman is so real
that for once her whole body has become a person
her hair is no longer jet-black
but she isn't sorry about her hair
she isn't unhappy she's frightened she's middle-aged
          she's a woman
she's beautiful
at this moment the picture of her destiny is shining clearly
          in her mind
she has endured a lot of her youth
now she's ready to walk bent over with age ahead of a man
in exchange for a little continuous affection
she knows a few hard-hearted men her husband knows
and she's convinced
he keeps her safe from them
she holds up her hand and stares at it
then combs out her hair with gentler strokes than before

Translated from the Hindi by Vinay Dharwadker

Preparations of War

After thousands of years
like the same beaten-up question
the same beaten-up man is still being asked
             'Who are you?
             Where do you live?
             What's your name?'

The prisoner who patrols
a motionless octagonal cell
holds three guards captive at the same time.

             Everywhere outside
             a forest of iron bars has spread its stranglehold
             like a magnet's invisible lines of force.

And this is the solid proof of the success
of a massive build-up of arms
that as soon as we have a gun in our hands
enemy heads
begin to appear all around us.

Translated from the Hindi by Vinay Dharwadker and Aparna
Dharwadker

White Paper

A great man once said to me:
write whatever you want to,
but on one condition—
it should be an improvement
on the blank white page.

Blank white paper
is more important
than what I write now.
My poetry
is in the white spaces
between the words.

Like news about the men
who disappeared before dawn,
like seeds buried in the soil,
like the truth that hides
between the heavy headlines,
like a fragrant green flower,
the more I write
the more poetry there is

in the white spaces between the words.

Translated from the Telugu by V. Narayana Rao

A Rat and a Sparrow

When she woke up and turned her face, the rat's face was right next to her cheek. When she screamed, jumped up and shivered, the rat also jumped up, assaulted by the scream, and cowered in the window. It lifted its nose as if to say, 'How you startled me with that scream!' Each time it tried to move, there was another scream. Finally, it sat down where it was, absolutely still. She stood there, staring at it, dazed.

It's hard to relate to rats. Especially to this rat. It must be this one that gnaws and eats only the autobiographies on the top shelf. Because some of the covers of the autobiographies have been eaten at random, without any method, some titles are left with remnants like MY AUTOB, MY ST, and MEMOI. In the book titled in big letters THE AUTOBIOGRAPHY OF A DONKEY, only the word DONKEY remained. When one looked at it from below, only the word DONKEY in thick dark print appeared under the smiling picture of the author. Though some people might think it's the right epithet for the author, it's not clear how far they would leave such judgments to a rat. It occurred to her that, though he might have referred to himself as a donkey in mock-humility, the author might still object to underlining it this way. Therefore, when she heard the *krk krk* sounds at night from the top shelf, she turned her flashlight on it. The rat had settled on the autobiography and had begun to gnaw around the donkey. It looked down at her. It seemed to smile at her. Her tongue twisted in a scream. Her friends who had celebrated their Saturday night with them in the usual way and had now fallen into a slumber, suddenly woke up. They chased away the two-inch rat. It ran and hid in the bathroom. Paramveer went in there with a coconut frond broom and shut the door behind him.

'Param, do not murder it. Just stun it.'

'It's only two inches long. How would I know how to stun it with the right blow?'

'What wilt thou do if it doth not perish after thou hast given it chase?' said Susan in high chaste Tamil. She had come from Paris. She was Param's girl-friend. She had come to India to research Hindu goddesses. She says that Lakshmi sitting at the feet of Vishnu and rubbing them is not a sign of male domination: it's only to give Vishnu the energy and enthusiasm he needs to create the world and to protect it. When she asked, 'If this Lakshmi has the power to rouse such fervour in the god, why doesn't she rub her own feet and do Vishnu's job herself?' Susan said, 'Thou art making me laugh,' in chaste Tamil. And now she stood there outside the bathroom, saying *aiyyaiyyo*! listening to the sounds of Param's struggles with the rat.

Param came out of the bathroom with the rat lying on its back on the coconut frond broom.

'It's just fainted,' he said to her. Then he went down to the street and let it go. When this Sardarji with his hair in a top-knot went down with a broom and a rat at one o'clock in the morning, the watchmen of the building were a little disturbed. Next day, they avoided looking at her directly.

Just when she was sleeping peacefully, imagining that the rat had recovered from its swoon and moved away to a world without autobiographies, right next to her cheek sat this rat.

Was it the same rat? Did it return here as soon as it recovered from its fainting fit? Or is this the other one's companion?

Several people had warned her that this big city had lots of rats and bandicoots. As these people were artists and intellectuals, there was good reason to think that they were describing human beings in this symbolic fashion. And then, here—in Gita's and Sukhdev's apartment with one room and a kitchen, the odour of pickles in mustard oil, mixed with the sweaty smells of clothes hanging on the clothesline—when she had to spend her first night in the city there with Amulyo, the rat image seemed quite appropriate. That kitchen did look like a rat-hole. She had a dream that night.

Buildings touching the sky on all four sides, like hills. Narrow streets. As you enter a building, looking for a place to live, the houses turn into rat-holes. Some people are lying on their backs, some on their sides. Some people are sleeping with their heads on their knees, some are talking, others are laughing. A woman comes home from her office, casually enters a rat-hole. In disembodied voices, they talk about the conveniences of their apartments. When she tried to hold on to a hanging rope in order to stand comfortably, she finds it's the rough-textured tail of a rat . . .

She must have uttered something in her sleep. She woke up. Amulyo was fast asleep. He had come into this world with the gift of sleep. She shook him.

'Amul . . . Amul . . .'

'Ha . . .' he said, startled, opening his eyes.

'Amul, I had a dream.'

'Mm.'

'It was a terrifying dream, Amul. My whole body went cold.'

Amul sat up and drank water from a bottle. He poured some into a glass and gave it to her. After she drank it, he said, 'Tell me.'

When she described it, he laughed.

'How is it you dream of such lovely images? Complete with symbols and all, and you don't even agree with Freud!'

She hit him in the stomach. 'You are a hooligan. You're a wretch. You're a sleepy head like Kumbhakarna. You're just an idiot.' With each epithet, she gave him another blow.

Laughing, he stretched and lay down. She climbed over him and sat on his stomach, her legs on either side of him, like a goddess about to slay a demon.

Amulyo held her uplifted hand. Quite gently. Her eyes filled. Amulyo's eyes also welled up.

Above their heads, shelves blackened by kitchen smoke. Aluminum vessels that could be discarded anytime they wished to pack up. A kerosene stove. Roach powder scattered along the edges of walls. Ten feet away, the kitchen drain. He looked at them and then at her and fell silent.

She softly played with his belly button.

'It was just a dream, Amul,' she said.

*

She remembered her Coimbatore house, its spaciousness, its backyard. Some places come twined with certain images. That house brought with it the image of Patti. Patti, who had borne children since she was thirteen. Patti who had cooked vegetables and sweet halvas in large frypans. Patti who had vigorously massaged her thin-fleshed grandchildren (she was also one among them) with castor oil and told them the *Ramayana* while she did so. Patti with a tongue like a whip. One word from her would sting like a lash.

Animals surrounded her, like cows around Krishna's flutesong.

Patti woke up suddenly from an afternoon nap one hot day. She went to the backyard. On the wall behind the well, a monkey was shrieking in a most horrible voice.

'Hey, what's the matter?' asked Patti.

'Urr,' it said.

Auntie's children cried out to her, 'Don't go near it, Patti!'

Patti stared at the monkey. She went to the woodpile next to the bathroom, and brought a coconut shell, dipped it in the cistern, filled it with water and went near the monkey. When she stretched out her hand with the shell, the monkey snatched it from her and drank up the water in one breath. She filled it again. The animal drank three times from her shell and darted away swirling its tail.

'It's thirsty,' said Patti.

The house had cats. Black, white, brown, at least a dozen cats. A line of granddaughters and grandsons. After feeding a line of the males first according to custom, she would sit down, stretching out a leg, to eat with a line of women, when the cats would come running.

'Meaow,' one would say.

'It wants a *papadam*,' Patti would translate. The cats had a taste for *papadam*, rasam, cooked rice, roast potatoes and so on. She would feed rice mixed with ghee to the cat that had just given birth to a litter and survived, poor thing. As soon as milk was delivered in the morning, the cats would get their share.

'Do you want a cat?' asked Amulyo.

'Unh, unh. Do you want one? You've a dog at home, don't you?'

'It's utterly wrong to shut up animals in these cage-like flats,' he said.

'Children too,' she added.

Since that dream about the rat, she had glimpses, *darshans*, of the rat, and heard rat legends. The rat experiences of Gita and Sukhdev. Once when they were watching a movie, munching on popcorn, something bit Gita in the leg. As she shook it off, Sukhdev also shook his leg. When they looked down, they saw a bandicoot running. Their feet were bloody. After several tetanus shots, he expressed his righteous indignation to a journalist friend of his, and asked him to write about it in his newspaper. The friend smiled most patiently and told Sukhdev what had happened to the film critic: when she missed the press showing of the movie, she went to see it in the regular theatre where it was playing. As she was making notes, she felt something tugging at her *dupatta**. She ignored it and continued to write on her pad resting it on the arm of the seat. When the lights came on at the intermission, she saw a rat in her lap. When she started up and let out a scream, people said, 'All this fuss about a rat!' The person next to her told a long elaborate rat joke. A woman learned judo. She also learned karate and *kalaripayirru*, the martial art of Kerala. But when she sighted a little mouse in her kitchen, she screamed and stood on a chair! The man who told the joke laughed like a hyena at his own joke. We don't know if any bandicoot had ever nipped at his foot.

She knew a story about a Rat Prince. Once upon a time, there were three princes. One of them was the Rat Prince. The other two drive him away. After several hardships, he meets a princess. As soon as she kisses him, he is transformed into a handsome young man . . . . She later added a footnote to the story, when she grew up. That kiss turned the rat into a prince. But the princess turned

---

* Dupatta: a long wrap worn around the neck.

into a rat. How weird! No prince ever came forward to kiss her, not even our Rat Prince.

After Gita and Sukhdev had gone away for a year, and these people had lived in that flat for a whole year, this rat had returned to do battle. Big cities usually have a symbol. Like the Big Apple for New York. The only symbol for this city, she thought, would be Rat. The city of rats. Rat people. Rat people who will still be rats even after a kiss. There might be a history to this rat cowering on the window. Maybe it had got tired of being a rat for ages, sick of eating all those autobiographies. Maybe it has come here all the way to kiss her and change himself into a prince.

She got up and pushed the windowpane out with a stick. The rat jumped out and ran.

When Amulyo returned from his trip the next day, she told him about the rat. Shall we buy rat poison? he asked her. This is such a literary rat, it shouldn't die in agony, she thought. There must be other ways to die. Come to think of it, she had a nonsensical praise-poem in her collection. A poem sung in praise of a leader in Tamil Nadu. His opponents in the party had spread a rumour that the poem had been sung in front of him a few hours before his death, that he had to be moved to the hospital soon after, and that the poem had something to do with it. She thought that this rat would surely die if it ate that poem. But would it writhe in agony? She felt like laughing.

'Do you happen to have a book that would finish it off?'

'Look here, don't you make fun of Tamil. Your books are so useless, even rats won't touch it.'

'Is this a border issue?'

'What else? How can an idiot who can't even pronounce a *zha* make fun of Tamil? Come say *Tamizh, Tamizh*, say *zh* let me see.'

Amulyo pronounced *zh* perfectly.

'Is it enough to pronounce it just once? Say *Vazhaippazham vazhukki kizhavi nazhuvi kuzhiyil vizhundal.** Say it.'

'Look here, I haven't slept all night in the train. I couldn't get

---

* In Tamil and Malayalam, the sound often written in English as *zh* (somewhat like an American r in words like card, or barn) is difficult for non-Tamils. Here Amulyo (obviously a Bengali by his name) is asked by his Tamil wife to utter a Tamil tongue twister which means, 'The old woman slipped on a banana and fell into a pit.'

a sleeper. First get me a cup of tea and then give me *Tamizh*—see I said *Tamizh*—then give me *Tamizh* lessons.'

They say this is a city where people of all kinds live. There was one big group labelled Madrasis. One of Amulyo's friends would make his mouth a little crooked whenever he saw her and say, 'Namaskaram ji.' He would grind that word pretty hard. He believed that adding *-am* to the end of any word would make it Tamil. So he would say, 'tea-*am*, coffee-*am*, chapatti-*am* . . .' in a drawled out list and ask, 'How's that?'

After he had done this once or twice, she said with great pity, 'Vijay, this speech defect of yours, have you had it from childhood? Is there any remedy for it? You have so much trouble speaking, poor thing!'

Vijay was startled. He stammered, 'No . . . . This . . . is Madrasi . . .'

'Oh, I was worried all these days that something was wrong with your tongue. You see, the rest of us don't speak like that.'

Vijay looked at Amulyo, as if asking for help.

'What, Vijay? What will you drink? Tea-*am*?'

Vijay said, in a small voice, 'Tea.'

Another friend, as soon as he had put away three good pegs of rum, had insisted on telling a joke. 'I'm going to act like a Madrasi,' he said in a loud voice. Before others could control him, he had become a Madrasi. 'I'm going to eat like a Madrasi,' he announced. He rolled up his sleeves, imagined he had a leaf full of food in front of him, scooped up a handful and sucked it in with a big hissing noise. Another big scoop of imagined food and another huge hiss of suction. Then he pretended he was filling his mouth noisily. Then he put out his tongue and pretended to lick the palm and then the back of his hand. Then he laughed at his own act, though no one else did.

Vijay went up to him and whispered something. He looked at her and said, grinning all the while, 'Just for fun . . . I love the temples in Tamil Nadu. I like the ddosa, vadda, iddli and all,' stressing the *dd*'s.

She said, 'Wretch!' in Tamil.

Only Amulyo understood what she said. He quickly gave his friend his bag and sent him home. Vijay didn't say as usual,

'Namaskaram ji,' but said 'Good night' to her, weakly, giving her a hug.

She was in a frenzy. She felt like embracing the plantain leaf seller in the Tamil-speaking colony of the city. When their Tamil dialect with words like *avuka* and *ivuka* fell on her ears, it felt as if the Tamraparni river itself had rolled over its banks. Tamil dishes like dosai, idli, vadai, rasam, idiappam, and the chicken curry of Chettinad seemed like the very staple of life. Forgotten Tamil songs began to appear in her memory suddenly at night, in the afternoon sun, or when wiping off sweat in the heat of buses and trains—it went through her like a lightning of pain. She heard her grandfather sing a folksong at night as he walked up and down the open terrace, looking up at the stars:

> *This rotting body, of no use for anything*
> *like a torn sieve—O parrot,*
> *it's forever a thing of pain.*

A frenzy possessed and shook her till she reached the Tamil bookstore. When she saw the colourful covers of books in the bookstore with their pictures of women looking up or lying down, her legs twined around themselves.

It looked as if the owner of the store would never remove his hand from within his *dhoti*. She couldn't think what great treasure was there inside. Whenever he saw a woman, his hand would go hide itself there. With the other hand, he spoke emphatically about Tamil culture.

'We're maintaining a culture, madam. I've been stoned in the cause of Tamil. (He pointed to a bald spot on his head.) We're now trying hard to put up a statue of Bharati and one of Tiruvalluvar[*]. I've proposed that we should inscribe stanzas from the *Kural*[**] all over the walls. As soon as you enter, your eyes should fall on a *Kural* stanza. It should pierce your eyes. You come in like this now. There should be a stanza:

[*] Subramania Bharati was a Tamil poet of this century and Tiruvalluvar a poet of the third or fourth century. Both are much loved by Tamils.
[**] *Kural*, or *Tirukkural*, is a work by Tiruvalluvar written in hemistichs, which are also called *kurals*.

Even if she doesn't worship a god,
if she worships her husband,
if she says, 'Rain?' it will rain.

'How do you like that? It would thrill you. We must praise our women. In our *Kural*- and *tevaram*-singing competitions, if a woman wins, we won't give her some random prize. We'll give her a brass lampstand, we'll give her a book on the place of women in Tamil culture.' Bending forward, he continued, 'Look, our entire culture is entirely in the hands of women.'

His voice was full of the satisfaction of having given over the entire culture into the hands of women. It occurred to her that if this man's hand would give up its cultural searches and come out, we could burden it also with a little of our culture.

Outside the bookstore, a man was speaking. He was a singer in the association where all South Indians came to learn the arts.

'They threw me out. You know that, don't you?'

'Is that so? Why?'

He quickly undid the buttons of his white starched shirt and showed his bare chest.

'I don't have a sacred thread.'

The two of them brought home a rather virulent rat poison. They spread it on pieces of bread and left them in corners. She put one piece behind *The Autobiography of a Donkey*. One couldn't tell which piece it ate. It lay peacefully dead inside the soft blue cotton bag. It touched her to the quick. Did it suffer agony, did it writhe? It spoiled her sleep. It ruined her books. It died alone writhing in the blue bag. Amulyo took it to the beach and shook it out.

This rat will no longer stand up to them, as the other one they saw once on the seashore. A man was walking in front of them with a rat-trap in his hand on the beach, one evening. There was a squealing little rat in it, looking through the trap. He opened the trap towards the sea. The rat was scared by the ocean. It refused to leave the trap. Squealing away, it grabbed the rods of the trap. He tried to shake the trap, turn it upside down, beat its sides. But the rat was obstinate, wouldn't come out. The man sat next to the trap, praying, waiting for the rat to come out. When she and Amulyo were leaving the beach, they looked back and found that the man was still sitting there, waiting. The rat didn't seem to appreciate his stubbornness. In the last light of the sunset, they saw the silhouette of the man and the rat-trap. Around the horizon stood buildings like hills.

*

The sparrow arrived some days after these events. When she stood in the veranda that was big enough only to hold one person, she looked first at the garbage heap below and the children sitting down in the road to defecate, and then turned to the old movie house in front. An old Hindi movie was running there. To compensate for the failure of the electric fans, they had opened all the balcony doors. Through the heavy black curtains, a song sung by Mukesh for Raj Kapoor floated towards her. It seemed to fall down, fluttering against her shoulders. Startled, she turned around: it was a sparrow. A little one. Its wing broken and crooked. Its mouth was red as a berry. She was afraid to touch it. She found an ink-filler, filled it with water, and dropped some in its mouth. It opened its eyes. She picked it up on cardboard and set it in a corner. At night she covered it with a net basket.

When she lifted the basket in the morning, the sparrow let out a chirp. With little squeaks, it turned in circles, and struck the ink-filler with its beak. Before she could turn, two sparrows had come and perched on the veranda parapet. They flew quickly down to the baby sparrow and inserted little grubworms into its mouth. The smart little one made appreciative chirping noises and swallowed them. Then it lay down.

Flying lessons began that very afternoon. One of the sparrows flew upwards, first slowly, then quickly. As soon as it sat down, the other one flew. The little sparrow tried to rise in the air with its crooked wing and fell down. Till five o'clock, both sparrows tried. The little one gave up on flying and began to walk. The sparrows left the little one in her care and left for the day. The little one couldn't fly more than five or six feet. It made its dwelling near the first iron bracket of the bookshelf. Unlike the stealthy rat that laid siege in the middle of the night, this one put droppings on one set of books even during the day. She kneeled one day in front of it and sang the old rhyme, 'Little sparrow, little sparrow, do you know, do you know, my man who has left me hasn't come home yet?' The sparrow made sharp *krk* noises and showed its displeasure. It also liked red things. It scattered its droppings freely on books with red covers. When she opened the door at night after a long absence, it squeaked from its corner and showed its disapproval.

When the window next to the bookshelf was opened, it went and perched on the cross bar. Against the background of buildings darkened by mill-smoke, and the smell and din of vehicles, a small crooked-winged sparrow was foregrounded. A little sparrow looking out of eyes like beads.

When a curtain of rain dimmed the outlines of everything, the sparrow was still on the bar. If one screwed one's eyes and looked at it sideways, the sparrow filled one's vision. Behind its head, there was a stretch of the ash-smeared city. As if it was placed on the sparrow's head. Like a crown.

When she leaned her head on the window and dozed off for a second and woke up, the sparrow wasn't there. She searched for it all over the flat, calling it, 'Little One, Little One.' When she called again loudly and looked out of the veranda, it showed its head from a hole in the building. She could see its crooked wing. Just when she was worrying how she would save it if a hawk or eagle or vulture should attack it, the little one rose lightly and flew out and returned to the hole in the wall. Then again it demonstrated how it could fly. When she and Amulyo stood in the veranda, it flew a third time rhythmically up and down and hid in the tree that was fifty feet away. There were many sparrows in that tree.

As far as the eye could reach, there were long rows of buildings, without any interval. Unfinished walls with cracks. On some curvy lines of cement over the cracks. Walls smeared with tar to keep them from getting soaked with rainwater. Colourful clothes hanging from long hooks attached to the verandas. In a few windows there were green leaves sprouting from planters. With all this, the city looked like a demon. In the middle of it all, in a tree that had somehow grown and branched out randomly, a little sparrow.

Then one evening something happened. Streetlights, shoplights, and neon ads had begun to shine. The road was a sea of vehicles. Double-decker buses roared by. Autorickshaws sliding and twisting noisily between them, impatient scooters and cars. It was a deluge of noises. Somehow Amulyo entered the stream, ran and scrambled on to the other side of the road. She got stuck on the one-foot stone division that cut the road in two. Amulyo summoned her to cross, making gestures with his hands. The eyes were mobbed by big bright posters stuck everywhere without wasting even a square foot. A double-decker bus passed, almost rubbing against her back. It was covered with monstrous patches of blue, green and black advertisements. Raging vehicles that screeched, came to a halt and then moved on. She took a couple of steps and retreated before a shrieking black car. Horn sounds drummed in her ear. Face, neck, armpits and thighs streamed with sweat. A woman clutching two empty fishbaskets in one hand approached her. The baskets reeked. With her one free hand, the woman caught her by the waist. Lifting her two baskets with one hand, signalling the traffic, she dragged her to the other side. Once she joined Amulyo, the fisherwoman moved on.

In that sidewalk filled with spittle, gutters, cigarette-stubs, and smalltime traders, overflowing with all the sounds of the city, while she stood for a second getting her breath back, the man came towards her. He would be called *bevda* ('drunk') in city lingo. The city treated *bevdas* with compassion. If a *bevda* lies down and sleeps in a bus or train, no one will wake him up. They would say, *bevda bevda*, and walk across forgivingly. Once, at midnight, a *bevda* boarded a bus and refused to buy a ticket from the conductor. He sputtered in Hindi, 'Drink drink drink. Drink in the morning, drink in the afternoon, drink at night. Drink drink drink.' The conductor himself bought a ticket for him. The man lay down with a thud, saying, 'Wake me up when we get to the temple.' There were temples all along the way. Every ten feet, there was a little Sai Baba shrine. At which temple should he be woken up? The conductor said, 'Poor fellow, *bevda*.'

When this *bevda* came in front of her, she saw that he was middle-aged. About ten feet away from her, he fell down on the sidewalk in 'slow motion.' No one noticed it. People walked around him.

When Amulyo and she went near him, he tried to get up but failed. Extending his index finger and thumb in a two-inch angle, he said, 'Had a little too much,' and smiled happily. They roused him a little from the sidewalk and made him lie down next to a wall. He said, 'Do I have my sandals on my feet? Could you hand them to me? The hooligans will snatch them and throw them away.' Once he had his sandals in his hand, he hugged them and shut his eyes. A peaceful smile on his face.

They stood in the long line at the bus stop. She leaned against the street lamp and started laughing. After a moment, Amulyo joined her. The two of them could not contain their laughter.

Translated from the Tamil by A. K. Ramanujan

S. *Usha*

To Mother

Mother, don't, please don't,
don't cut off the sunlight
with your sari spread across the sky
blanching life's green leaves.

Don't say: You're seventeen already,
don't flash your sari in the street,
don't make eyes at passers-by,
don't be a tomboy riding the winds.

Don't play that tune again
that your mother,
her mother and her mother
had played on the snake-charmer's flute
into the ears of nitwits like me.
I'm just spreading my hood.
I'll sink my fangs into someone
and lose my venom.
Let go, make way.

Circumambulating the holy plant
in the yard, making *rangoli** designs
to see heaven, turning up dead
without light and air,
for god's sake, I can't do it.

---

* Rangoli: floor designs.

Breaking out of the dam
you've built, swelling
in a thunderstorm,
roaring through the land,
let me live, very different
from you, Mother.
Let go, make way.

Translated from the Kannada by A. K. Ramanujan

The Slant

This slanting light at four o'clock.
On the tiled roof,
with the eye of a palmist,
the cawing crow, head aslant.

Alongside the crow
its shadow also sits—
sits at a slant.

In the courtyard
like a trembling hand
the slanting shadow of the coconut frond.
In my room
the thin shadows of the window bars,
they too lie aslant.

Outside the gate
a stranger walking along,
the sound of his footsteps—
why is it slanted?
The forecast of the crows
the soughing of the seabreeze
the footsteps of the passer-by—
why are they slanted?

I've become suspicious.

Finally,
on my table
on its own axis
I saw the earth slant
but I sit straight
in front of it.
On this slanting earth
where everything is slanted
why is it
I alone am straight?

Translated from the Malayalam by Ayyappa Paniker and Arlene Zide

Mitro Marjani*

When Suhagwanti emerged from calming down her parents-in-law, she noticed the two brothers through the doorway. Seeing them lost in thought, she shrank back and entered her own room. She said to Mitro, 'Sister, what is all this commotion about? Why don't you do what your husband tells you?'

Mitro looked first at her husband and then ogled Banwari mischievously, 'Ah, my sensible sister-in-law! What do you know about love and love-making?'

Unable to listen to any more, Banwari grabbed his brother's hand and dragged him out, saying, 'Suhag, put Mitro to bed in your room.'

As the brothers shut the door to the next room behind them, Mitro slapped her forehead and laughed out loud, 'Idiots, they can't think straight! If they were real men, they would lick at me greedily, or snap me up raw like lions!'

Suhag did not look at her. She pulled up the charpoy and spread the quilt on it, then said, 'It's really late, Mitro. Why don't you forget these worries and problems and get some rest?'

Mitro made a face at her, 'What worries and problems? I wasn't born from the womb of a mother who worried!'

Chee, chee! Suhag's ears were burning as she listened. Mitro got up and came near the bed. First she picked up the quilted cover and ran her fingers over the thick woven mat, then felt around the pillows and said, 'Suhag, there can't be anyone as mad as your brother-in-law, he just has his head screwed on the wrong way. No

---

* Excerpted from the novel, *Mitro Marjani*.

happiness, no sorrow, no love, no romance, neither thirst nor burning—just beatings and fights every day, curses and accusations!'

Suddenly a sort of wild intoxication shone through her eyes. She pulled the *dupatta* off here neck. Then she took off her long *kurta** and *salwar*** and flung them aside. Laughing, she said, 'Banwari says, Mitro, it's not a body you have there, it's sugar, pure su-gar! I tell that wretch— "This is sugar, sugar which breeds an army of poisonous snakes to sting your life away!"'

Suhag's face was dark with mortification. She clapped her hands over her ears and said, 'I beg you, sister, don't make me a partner to sin.'

Mitro lay down flat on the bed in a flash. She did not cover herself. Suhag felt as if sharp needles were pricking her all over her body. If a woman has no decency, like this walking disgrace to family honour, her body becomes ever more polluted, a house for sin itself. She pulled the quilt over her head, covering her face.

She heard Mitro call out to her, 'Just open your eyes for a minute and look this way, please, Suhag.'

Suhag scolded her through the covers, 'Those brothers have awfully big ears, Mitro. If they hear you . . . '

Lying there, Mitro said flippantly, 'If they hear me, so what? I'm not afraid of them.' Then she pleaded with her sister-in-law, 'Listen to me just this once, please!'

Suhag opened her eyes, annoyed, and raised her head, 'Now what?'

Her sister-in-law sat up from the bed. Propping up her breasts with both hands, engrossed in them, she asked innocently, 'Tell me true, Suhagwanti, have you ever such breasts on any other woman?'

Suhag's entire body started to burn. She threw the covers aside and hit her forehead with both hands, exclaiming, 'You little so and so, after you die no one will know that you ever existed! What are you so proud of, this woman's body? It melts away, day and night, into nothingness. Damn you! There are disgraceful women like you

---

* Kurta: a loose shirt.
**Salwar: baggy pants.

in every house. They have two hands just like you, two eyes, and yes, breasts just like yours! Are you the only one with a woman's organs?'

Mitro spread her arms wide without any shame, 'I'd even die for my prim and proper sister-in-law! But at least tell your man that Mitro won't leave the world while she still has this God-given power.'

Good-natured Suhag drew herself up like a demon-goddess in battle, 'Quiet, you godless tart! Put your clothes on, or else . . . '

Mitro grinned when saw Suhag angry and pulled her clothes on. Suhag shook her head and continued, as if speaking to herself, 'Immoral! We brought her here a properly married bride, and she carries on like a slut. Goddess of lights, keep this house's reputation clean!'

She looked at Mitro, 'Sister-in-law, your luck was bad today—you escaped these two brothers. If anything serious had happened to you, then you'd finally be free of this tangle and they'd be happy too.' Then, putting her hand on her chin, she asked grimly, 'Tell the truth, now, how did you get to be so sinful?'

Mitro did not draw back or hesitate. Lying there, she said, 'There's no river my mother has not crossed, she's as black as the bottom of an old cooking pot. And I was born, whiter than driven snow, from her womb. She used to say that Mitro is the gift of the big landowner of the district. Now you tell me, where could I get such a power of virtue as you? Your brother-in-law doesn't recognize my disease. At most he approaches me once a week or once a fortnight—and my body is so thirsty it thrashes around like a fish out of water!'

Suhag stared at her through eyes opened wide, as if she were seeing her for the first time, as if she could not remember what her face looked like. She shook her head and said in a tight little voice, 'Mitro, your mother did something very wrong when she deceived these decent people.' Then her mouth trembled and she burst out, 'For a daughter or daughter-in-law, the ways of her home and household are like the line that Lakshman drew around Sita. Knowingly or unknowingly, if this line is ever breached . . . '

Mitro put her hands over her ears. Her eyes shone with mischief, 'You can beat a moral lesson into me and I'll nod and agree, Suhag, but the desire that overcomes my body . . . '

The scandalized Suhag could not listen to any more. She said warningly, 'That's enough, Mitro!'

Laying her head back on the pillow, Mitro closed her eyes and reasoned with herself, 'Mitro Rani! Let your enemies worry! God shaped you and sent you into this world to enjoy your pleasures, so God will do all the worrying for you. Why fret?'

The local policeman's face swam before her closed eyes. Niamat Rai was tall and handsome, with big moustaches. At first he would just stand by her and grin and laugh, then one day he said harshly, 'Princess, sit up straight! Don't you know I'm here?'

'As far as I am concerned, you're a thieving rascal! Niamat Rai, this is my kitchen, not your police station.'

Niamat reached out and pulled her *dupatta* away, 'Yes, yes, we've heard enough. You'll just lie here and your kitchen will be robbed.'

Happily, Mitro sat up and spread her arms out, 'You are disgraceful! When a tomcat sees cream, he comes rushing to lick it up.'

As she fell back on the quilt, Suhag scolded her again, 'Go to sleep and don't let your imagination run away with you. If I see you moving again . . . '

Annoyed, Mitro muttered away to herself. She wanted to say, Suhag, do you have any control over that whoremaster you worship as your husband? But then she thought, my sister-in-law must be on the right track, all religious and everything. Else how would she know I was conversing with Niamat Rai just lying here?

At dawn, Mitro opened her eyes to find her mother-in-law sitting by her instead of Suhag. The previous night's events came back to her. She sat up and stretched lazily. Then she stared teasingly at Dhanwanti, saying with her eyes: Mother-in-law, I didn't beg or borrow my prime from somebody else!

Impudently she asked, 'Up so early, *amma*?* Is poor Mitro going to the next world, have you come to light her way there?'

Dhanwanti stared at her daughter-in-law sadly for a few moments, then shook her head in refusal, 'Why would an

---

* Amma: mother.

unfortunate old woman like me have such good luck? If your husband had put you on your funeral pyre after a respectable life, then I'd mourn my Sumitrawanti honestly. But my luck is terrible. No, I wasn't fated to see that day.'

'There'll be lots of days, yet, *amma*. Why finish off all the worrying and mourning today?'

Hearing Suhag call from the kitchen, Dhanwanti rose and slapped her forehead in despair, 'A million curses on me, Mitro! Why did I ever get mixed up with your mother?'

Mitro was about to retort when she saw her elder brother-in-law's tall shadow on the threshold and held herself back. Remembering the previous night, she made a play of veiling herself and called out naughtily, 'Of course I'm nothing compared to my dear sister-in-law, but still you might look this way occasionally . . . ?'

Deliberately not hearing her, Banwari Lal turned back and Suhag came into the room, 'Mitro, I've already had a quick bath. Phoolan is not feeling well, so I'll sweep out the house and courtyard and you take care of the kitchen.'

'Suhag, I'm so devastated! Every day that grocer's daughter Phoolan stages some new drama. All she wants by day is four plates of sweets, and at night some *jalebis** in a pint of warm milk will do nicely.'

Suhag shook her head, 'No, don't accuse her falsely, there's something wrong with her body.'

Mitro's eyes shone, 'Oh, yes, one day she breaks a bone, the next day her head is splitting, on the next she has a backache, today her heart . . . '

Suhag reproached her, 'Phoolan is really sick today. Her body is all hard, like solid wood.'

'Darling Phoolan, what times these are for her! How would she ever live up to her family name if she were absolutely hale and hearty? A solidly-built girl like her, she'd share out the groceries so that a man would never know what hit him. I don't think her husband even knows when she gets her periods!'

---

* Jalebi: fried sweets dipped in syrup.

Suhag wanted to laugh out loud, but kept a serious face and coaxed, 'Get up, my sister, go and bathe quickly.'

Mitro jumped up enthusiastically, as if it were her sixteenth birthday. Seeing her husband in the courtyard, she held herself even more proudly, 'Still here, love—I haven't passed away yet.'

Sardari just grimaced at her angrily in reply. Casually dismissing him with her hand, she frowned and said, 'Damn it, why on earth should I make up with him?'

And then she took herself into the bathhouse.

When she emerged, all washed and clean, her elder sister-in-law was in the kitchen, frying *paranthas** on the griddle. Mother-in-law was sitting with her sons in father's room, cooking up some other muddle.

Swinging her hips merrily, Mitro went on into Phoolan's room. Her younger sister-in-law had returned to consciousness. Phoolan's husband, Gulzari Lal, sat there rubbing her palms to rouse her.

Mitro was laughing inside, but she made a great show of concern and said caressingly, 'Oh! Phoolan, my dear, such dreadful diseases, at such a young age! This lying around unconscious, it's a terrible thing, it sucks all the blood out of your body.'

Phoolan looked at Gulzari reproachfully and then stretched out a pathetically weak arm, 'Mitro, my sister, no one listens to me! I've given up on telling them my true disease. I have no spirit left, no strength at all, but everyone thinks I'm lying here shamming. How can I explain that I'm suffering from palpitations?'

'Palpitations! You're not serious, are you? That's the most vicious thing, the king of diseases!' Looking at her brother-in-law she said, 'Gulzari Lal, don't go to work today—find a cure for my poor sister here, or you might lose a beautiful young wife.'

Gulzari Lal could not figure out whether Mitro was giving them good advice or being sarcastic. He just stared at her dumbly.

Phoolan struck at him from her spine position, 'Who cares whether I live or die?'

Mitro came near her and placed a hand on Phoolan's chest.

---

* Paranthas: fried bread.

She shook her head ruefully and said, 'It's astonishing, have you heard her heart? It's palpitation all the way to the sky, just listen . . .'

Gulzari Lal went pale. Stammering, he asked, 'Is it really serious?'

'Serious? Gulzari Lal, nobody ever escapes from palpitations. It's a fatal disease, it kills whoever it affects. Give your princess good medicine, ground pearls and rare pickles, and take her to the best doctor in town for treatment.'

Gulzari reached out and touched Phoolan's arm, but she began to cry in great noisy sobs, 'Nobody escapes palpitations! I'm dying, somebody call a doctor!'

At first Mitro stood and watched her, then winked at Gulzari and clapped loudly, 'Wonderful performance, Phoolan, I have to admit! Gulzari, your precious bride has no palpitations, no pain, and no weakness. All these acts are only skin-deep. Don't just keep looking at her like a nitwit, Gulzari, one day she'll make off with your brains, the thief!'

Phoolan roared full-throatedly, like a wounded lioness, 'Those who call my sickness a lie, beware! May their souls and eyes ache, may their hearts split with pain!'

Mitro scolded, 'Shut up, Phoolan! Why don't you give up these false diseases? Produce a son for your man!'

Seeing that the sparring did not stop, Dhanwanti entered the room. She glared at her two daughters-in-law and reproached her son, 'Gulzari, why are you letting them carry on like this? Listen to this rubbishy quarrelling! Mitro cannot control her tongue, but at least you could have stopped your own wife.'

Gulzari shook his head helplessly, exclaiming in a hurt tone, 'If it were Phoolan's fault, I could tell her off. But when our elder sister-in-law comes and starts throwing taunts around herself . . .'

Twisting her mouth, Mitro retorted 'So it's criticism now, is it? I would have thought, Gulzari Lal, that when they equipped you with a wife you'd have become a man . . .'

Dhanwanti cut Mitro off angrily, 'Don't talk like a whore in the house! Hold your tongue!'

Mitro ran her eyes over her brother-in-law's body, then teased, 'Gulzari, are you so scared of mother's little talks? You're a fine young man, what does Phoolan do with you anyway?'

Thorns prickled all over Dhanwanti's body, 'Get out of my sight, Mitro!' And she covered her eyes with her hand.

Mitro merely held herself a finger's breadth higher. She saw that her mother-in-law would not open her eyes, and said, '*Amma*, open your eyes and look at me! Do you think I'll go away just because of a little scolding?'

Dhanwanti turned towards Phoolan and asked with concern, 'Are you feeling any better, my dear? Have you eaten anything?'

'I'm just fine, mother, what could be wrong with me? I have no sickness at all, I'm just staging a play lying here.'

Dhanwanti understood that she was repeating Mitro's taunts and tried to explain, 'Phoolan, she does keep teasing people, but she has no idea about what's proper and what's not all right to say. How can you pay any attention to her?'

Phoolan's anger reached flash point, 'I know full well who spoils her, *amma*! She can say whatever she wants, no one at all can stop her.'

Mitro teased her sister-in-law some more, 'Phoolan, my queen, showing our innocent mother how poisonously you can sting? Enjoy yourself every night, but be sure to stage the *Mahabharat* in the morning.'

Dhanwanti continued to placate Phoolan, '*Bahu*,* don't talk to Mitro. Eat a little something, get some rest.'

Phoolan was in torments despite the kind words, 'Tell someone else all these sweet stories, *amma*! Ever since I entered this house, I haven't been able to live freely. You're all jealous of me because my brothers are rich merchants . . .'

Mitro winked naughtily at her younger brother-in-law, 'Oho, Princess Phoolan, why stop at rich merchants, why don't you say they are kings and emperors?' Then she smiled sweetly and addressed her again, 'Tons of dried goods, tons of wafers, isn't that the trade at your father's grocery?'

Phoolan got out of bed and sat down with a crash. Shooting a burning glance at her husband, she banged her head against the bed-frame again and again and cried loudly, 'I know you're all

---

* Bahu: daughter-in-law.

against me, you won't let me live in this house! All you want is my jewellery!'

Dhanwanti trembled with rage and humiliation, 'Phoolan, have you lost your mind?'

Phoolan appealed to Gulzari Lal, 'You can see it with your own eyes, how your mother and brother's wife torture me. They want to rip me up and eat me alive! I've been patient till today, but you can take it from me—I won't leave my ornaments, all my jewels!'

Dhanwanti could barely speak, 'Daughter, don't you trust me? It's living death for me, if in our house everything becomes a question of yours and mine. Aren't we family?'

'It's not a question of who's family and who's not, mother. Why don't you say something about my jewellery?'

Dhanwanti looked at Gulzari Lal for help, 'Son, she's so brazen! In front of you! Why don't you explain things to her?'

Gulzari did not look at this mother. Without saying anything, he got up and left the room.

Seeing her son avoid the issue, Dhanwanti herself weakened. Controlling her anger, she said in a sensible tone, 'Phoolan, my girl, we brought the heavy gold cuffs left by Banwari's first wife as part of your wedding portion, so what crime did I commit by giving some of your jewellery to Suhag? Phoolanwanti, all the parts of a household fit together. Such grudges and quarrels don't befit a good *bahu*.'

But Phoolan was angry, and stood ready to fight, 'Why should anyone take away the gold and clothes given to me by my mother? Why share them out? They aren't here to be plundered!'

Dhanwanti was silenced. She shook her head and said, 'Have some shame, *bahu*. What will the neighbours say if they hear you?'

'As far as I am concerned, let the whole world hear. Why should a woman whose jewels are being robbed hold her tongue?'

Mitro nodded, enjoying herself hugely. She patted her sister-in-law on the back and said, 'Well done, Phoolan! What a wonderful thing to say about a grey-haired old woman! You know, princess, if I were your husband's mother, I wouldn't leave a single hair standing on your stupid little head!'

Phoolan's mind was boiling with rage. She wanted to scratch Mitro's hair out by the roots, but suddenly she thought of

175

something else and became sad. Seating herself on the bed, she said darkly, 'Whoever cares for her self-respect should move on, be on her way. I don't want to trip anyone up, no one should mess with me.'

Mitro continued as a spectator, looking by turns at the two women. Then she laughed, 'Phoolan, my queen, I may be notorious as absolutely the worst there is, but darling, you're earning a good solid name for yourself.'

Dhanwanti felt a wave of affection for Mitro. So what if I am always cursing her and scolding her, at least she has the grace to side with her mother-in-law. Shaking her head, she said, 'Daughters-in-law, please forgive me for whatever I said. I didn't know that I'm not the mother in this house, just a servant—a servant!'

Mitro felt real pity for her mother-in-law, but she put on a teasing tone, '*Amma*, mothers have been servants to their children since the beginning of time, but under what name are you going to worship this little bride of yours? If I had my way, I'd set up a temple to Phoolan Dear instead of Krishna!'

Suhag had been sitting far away, watching the war of words. At last she gave up and came to them, saying angrily, '*Amma*, do you have to listen to this two-bit, worthless rubbish? Will your life go to waste otherwise?'

Seeing Suhag escorting Dhanwanti away, Phoolan called out from behind, 'Yes, sister, might as well take her off with you, since you're going to inherit everything anyway. At least you could be kind enough to return my jewellery!'

Suhag turned and marched back to Phoolan, telling her off in a low, serious tone, 'Sister, forget all this sarcasm and taunting for a minute. Have you sworn to leave nothing sacred in this house?'

Phoolan did not tremble, 'Why should I hold anyone sacred whose intentions are bad? You get me back what I brought in my dowry, three suits of clothes, a heavy brocade wrap from Benares, jewellery and one gold head-ornament, and I have no grudges against anyone!'

'Phoolanwanti! All the grudges are in your mind. I won't inherit the realm if I keep your miserable little trinkets and clothes.

You should understand that these are the ways of a family which lives together.'

Phoolan taunted sarcastically, 'That's great! Those who can rob someone else's stuff just sitting at home understand "the ways of the family" very well, but for the poor wretches who lose everything it's highway robbery!'

Suhag felt genuinely sorry for her, 'Now, little sister, all this impertinence is not proper.'

'You've asked the right question, let's discuss proper and improper. Where is the line of propriety drawn? All the stuff that my mother gave me, tell me whose it is by right?'

Suhag did not flinch. She left instantly and brought the two pieces of jewellery back, 'Here you are, Phoolan, take your things.'

Phoolan hid the happiness she felt in her heart. Taking the ornaments, she turned them up and down in her hand. To Suhag she said, 'Since there's been so much water under the bridge already, why don't you just return my clothes as well? That'll put an end to the whole quarrel.'

Mitro jumped in, all sweetness and light, 'Phoolan, will this running sore ever stop flowing? Take it from me—till your heart remains greedy, you'll always be screaming and fighting in these arguments, princess!'

Suhag retreated from the room. Mitro winked mischievously and teased, 'Congratulations, Phoolan! Today, you've won the war. We should celebrate—beat a drum, give out halva and puris with your own hands!'

Phoolan endured all of Mitro's taunts silently, and waited patiently and hopefully for Suhag's return. Finally, seeing her precious clothes lying on Suhag's arm, she was so happy it seemed she had visited all the seven great pilgrimage sites successfully.

But Mitro stopped Suhag in the middle of the room and snatched the clothes away, 'Now, sister, I'll settle accounts with her!'

Suhag scolded, 'Why don't you let her have them, Mitro, do you want to start another war?'

Mitro shook her head, 'Not once but a thousand times. This greedy girl has gone mad over these clothes, as if her ancestors won't cross over to heaven without them!'

Then she addressed Phoolan naughtily, 'Forget about these, little sister! You can take them back in the afterlife!'

Phoolan frowned at her, as if she could scare Mitro with her eyes alone, 'I'll see how she won't return them!'

And, with her eyes alone, Mitro answered, 'No . . . never!'

Phoolan assessed Mitro carefully, then began to plead with her, 'Sister, when Suhag was going to return them to me anyway, then who are you to jump in?'

'I'm your personal devil from hell! You fought with our mother-in-law and I accepted it, but now you want to drag Suhag's honour down into the mud. You're not worth the sole of one of her shoes. Put those ornaments away quietly, or you'll lose those as well!'

Phoolan was about to reply, but became still when her sister-in-law hummed menacingly. Quietly she tied the jewellery up in the corner to her *dupatta*, then sat down on her bed.

Mitro put all the clothes back in Suhag's hands, 'Swear to me by the ten Gurus, sister-in-law, that you won't return the clothes to her. Better to give them to some pauper than to this no-good wretch.'

Flushed and triumphant from war, Mitro turned and re-entered her own room.

Translated from the Hindi by Aditya Behl

The Husband Speaks

This house is mine
I've touched you
Kissed you
Felt and enjoyed you
That's why I keep you here.

This house with its marble floor
Decorated with fine furniture
A roof above,
Walls on every side
A kitchen nearby
And there a living-room.
You cook my food,
Get your two meals from me.

This home is filled with lively children
Blood of my blood, they'll use my wealth
Hallow my name
And perpetuate my lineage.
Propitiating my spirit
They'll provide food for me
In the next world, if not the present.

You mothered my children,
So you enjoy the status of a lady;
If I held back my claim
To fatherhood, you'd lose
Your claim.
You belong to me
Wholly and truly you are mine. I
Own all that is yours.

Well,
For me it's different
I'm your husband.

Translated from the Sindhi by the poet with editing by Arlene Zide

Maami

I can hear the women wailing in the house across the street. Maami is dead.

I wonder who the people are who are wailing? Which women? Because nobody ever bothered about Maami while she was alive. She was always like a discarded rag. It was only her own eyes which shed tears for her plight. She cried so much, during the early flush of her youth, during the midday of her life, during the lingering shadows of her ebbing years, throughout her life. Eventually her tears dried up, and the bitterness leapt like flames in her veins.

Who is wailing for her today?

I feel angry.

So would Maami be, if she could hear them wailing so loudly around her dead body. If she could get up, she would pull away her shroud and sit up on her bed, with her hunchback, and look scornfully at the wailing women.

Her face looked like a crumpled piece of paper, thrown carelessly in the wastepaper basket. At such moments, when she felt suffocated in that house, she came to my mother, walking with the help of a stick which looked as old as Maami herself, dragging her legs, shifting her weight from one painful foot to the other, walking in a zigzag way because all her joints ached.

Sometimes when she didn't find my mother at home, she simply stood in the middle of the street and didn't know where to go.

But today she has gone, forever.

181

I am not crying. I think I am not sorry for her death, I was sorry for her when she was alive. Not now, no more!

I don't know how old she was. I had always seen her like that—a little hunchback, short and crumpled, walking with the help of a worn-out stick, cheeks sunken in, chin almost touching the tip of her nose because she had lost all her teeth. When she walked, she looked like an old toy which moves when you wind it up. It seemed all the nuts and bolts had come loose. A little nudge and the arms and legs would come apart like broken twigs, and the body would open up like a dry bean.

Early in the morning, before anybody else got up, she would drag her dust-laden slippers to the Sikh gurudwara and then to the temple. We could hear her stick tapping on the street in the still, pre-dawn hour. But neither the gods living in the temple nor the one living in the gurudwara ever came to her rescue.

She belonged to the city where my mother's parents lived before Partition. Gujranwala. After Partition, we had drifted to Delhi and so had Maami's family. It was a coincidence that our houses were opposite each others' in this resettlement colony of Patel Nagar.

Though it was a resettlement colony, people had yet to settle down. It is difficult to take root all over again in unknown, alien soil. In their shared grief they felt close to each other, though. And when Maami once told my mother about her family, my mother discovered that the branches of our family trees had intertwined somewhere in the remote past. That's why my mother started calling her Maami, and so did everyone else in our house, even us children. And later on she became Maami to the whole street.

She would often come to my mother complaining about that 'other woman.' 'You are like a daughter to me,' she told my mother, 'that's why I am telling you, otherwise who has the time to listen to my woes? And how can I disclose my family troubles to an outsider?'

'Of course, Maami, I am like your own daughter,' my mother reassured her.

'Look, that woman says I shouldn't enter the kitchen when she is serving food to her children. Isn't that treacherous? Who brought these children up, I ask you? Who washed their soiled nappies? Who always cooked for them? Who took them to their schools and brought them back home? Even now I wash all their clothes. Till yesterday I was even cleaning the utensils. Now that I can't sit at the tap, she's got a part-time maid to clean the kitchen.'

'Of course, Maami, you have slaved for them throughout your life. Who doesn't know that?' my mother reassured her again, trying to calm her down a bit.

'They are my children, more mine than anybody else's. She has just kept them inside her body for nine months. But I have served them ever since. For years and years. And now she says I would look at their food with hungry eyes, and it would harm them.'

'Why do you bother? It gives you time to relax. Let her do the cooking.'

'Yes, of course. Let her cook. But she doesn't know what the children like. She doesn't make what they like. Sinder likes *paranthas* stuffed with grated radish. He likes what I make fried in fresh butter. She doesn't know.'

'Maami, make those stuffed *paranthas* for me. I'll eat them,' I said.

'Of course I'll make nice *paranthas* for you, my angel,' she smiled and looked like a small child, happy and contented. 'Do you have fresh radish?' she asked my mother, suddenly full of excited enthusiasm.

'Relax, Maami. She is just . . .'

But Maami wouldn't listen. She would spend the next hour, fluttering vigorously in the kitchen, frying fresh and crisp *paranthas*. Her face looked transformed. Wrinkles disappeared. Back straightened up. Her skin glowed.

'Who is "that woman" she talks about?' I asked my mother.

My mother always avoided my question. Said, children shouldn't listen to adult talk. Said, children should sit down and read their books quietly.

When I grew up a bit, I gathered together all the loose threads of Maami's story.

A very ordinary story. One might find it bizarre and even boring. But that's how life is. Bizarre and boring.

She got married when she was sixteen.

On the wedding night her husband removed her veil, saw her face, and quietly walked out of the room. The room which is called the 'bridal chamber.' He told his parents that it was only a daughter-in-law they had brought home. He wouldn't take her as his wife. She was too repulsive, he said.

Maami was dark-skinned. That was her only blemish, her only fault.

She was a married woman, and yet not married. She had a husband, and yet she didn't.

She went to her parents. Her brothers and their wives didn't accept her. They had married her off, therefore she didn't have a right to live under their roof. Her parents also sided with the sons though her mother cried for her daughter. The father said she should go and adjust with the in-laws, otherwise society would besmirch the fair name of their family.

She went back to her in-laws. The mother-in-law said, 'If my son doesn't accept you, you have no place in this house.'

And she was kicked like a ball from her parents' house to her in-laws' place, and back. A ball which has no air in it, and no bounce.

And then her husband decided to remarry. So he got her a small hovel for two rupees a month and shoved her there. She was told to come to her husband's house on the first of every month and collect ten rupees for her maintenance.

'But why? Why did she agree to be humiliated like this?'

'What else could she do? She was not educated. She couldn't go out and earn her living by doing odd jobs. If she did, her brothers would have killed her. Or her husband. They couldn't allow their family names to be tarnished by an unwanted woman,' my mother said in a tone which was wet with grief, yet rather matter-of-fact as though that was the only possibility even she could visualize. As though nothing better was possible; nothing else could be done.

'Ten rupees a month!' I couldn't believe it.

It went on for years.

The husband married again, produced children. The children grew up. And Maami grew tired and old.

And then, when the shadows started lengthening, her husband died. The husband's second wife refused to pay her monthly allowance, saying, 'The one who promised you the maintenance is dead. He hasn't left any instructions for you. Why should I waste my money on you? Who are you after all? I don't know you.'

But then the relatives intervened. And the neighbours said, what will the poor woman eat? How will she live?

The second wife said, 'Well, she can shift to this house. She can cook and clean and do the household work, and she will get her food.'

So she moved in. Into the house from where she had been turned out. Into the house she wasn't allowed to enter throughout her life.

She moved in and replaced the servant whose services were terminated.

Looked after the buffalo, milked it before anyone else got up. Churned the yogurt and took out white balls of butter. Cooked, cleaned, washed. Even pressed the other woman's feet and massaged her head.

The only thing which gave her pleasure was when she made special dishes for the children. All these years she had forgotten how to cook any dishes. What could she cook for herself on that meagre allowance of ten rupees a month where she lived in that hovel, alone? Now all her cooking skills came back to her from across all those long years, and she felt milk slowly circling in her shrivelled breasts when she saw the children eating with relish what she cooked for them.

Gradually the children got married and moved away. Only the youngest, Sinder—his real name was Surinder, but everybody called him Sinder—was not yet prepared to get married. He wanted to get settled in his career first. He was working in Bombay and used to come home about twice a year.

My mother had gone across the street to where Maami was lying in a peaceful sleep. I knew my mother wouldn't cry loudly along with those wailing women, because my mother's grief was deep and genuine.

I wanted to be near my mother in her loneliness, because deep pain makes one very lonely. I walked across and peeped in.

Before I could go and sit with my mother, that other woman whom everybody called Chhoti Maami whispered to me, 'Jeet, Sinder is sitting in his room. I don't know what has happened to him. Since morning he is sitting there and refuses to talk to anyone. Can you go and persuade him to have something to eat? At least he could have a cup of tea.'

I went back to our house and put some snacks in a plate and a glass of buttermilk. I covered both the things with napkins so that the neighbours wouldn't see. People are not supposed to eat or drink while a dead body is lying in their house.

I went straight to Sinder's room. He was sitting there, with a bewildered look on his face.

I placed the plate of snacks and the glass of buttermilk on a small table near him, and said softly, 'Sinder Veer, I've brought this for you. Have a little bite.'

He looked bewildered and terrified. And then his face relaxed. He looked at me for a moment, and then took my hand, put his forehead on it and started crying like a child.

Between sobs he told me, 'Jeet, I don't know what happened. I came by the night train. Reached here early morning. Went straight to elder mother's room. She was lying there on her bed. For the last few years she had been asking me for a thick woollen shawl. Every time I came home she would say, "Sinder, you haven't bought me anything from your first salary. Buy me a shawl. I feel very cold in winter." But in Bombay you don't get good shawls. This time one of my friends had gone to Kashmir. I gave him money to buy one of the best pieces for her. I entered her room. She saw me and her face glowed with happiness. She got up and showered me with her blessings, caressing my head with a trembling hand.

'And then I took out the shawl. Opened it up, and covered her with it. She looked exultant, laughed like a child, blessed me, caressed the shawl with her hands, looked at it, and suddenly fell back on the bed.

'I called out to her. Touched her. She still looked as if she was laughing, but her pulse had vanished. I ran out and brought a doctor. He said she was dead.

'Did that shawl kill her, Jeet? Did I kill her with that shawl?'

'No, Sinder Veer, she died of love and happiness,' I said softly.

Translated from the Punjabi by the author

Ketaki Kushari Dyson

After the Rain Has Ended

After the rain has ended, in the shimmering silk sky
The trembling leaves are beginning to talk with the rainy wind,
The sound of evening traffic comes from the wet highway,
And music falls now and then from lighted windows.

Coming home from the restaurant, I see above the church's
steeple
The full moon that has risen, white as a conch shell.
A sliver of moonlight has come to stay in my empty bed,
And the walls are washed with the rhythm of the clock.

Ten-fifteen at night—the brightly lit station—sadness—
It keeps me awake, it is in the depths of my memory—
a face framed in a window—the muffled roar as the train begins
                                                    to move.
Desire, like the high tide when it comes in, has filled me.

The wave marks the shore where it returns;
Ten days without a letter, without a sight of you.

Translated from the Bengali by Leslie Minot and Satadru Sen

Avatars

when he reads
smutty books
that foul the waters
a contagion
in the depths of society
and smacks his lips over them
in his own room
all alone

he's the Fish

when he shrinks within his own shell
and hides himself
as others call upon him
to do good, strong deeds

he's the Tortoise

when he falls flat on his face
in an ocean of booze
and eagerly creates
a singular sort of world

he's the Pig

at the office
when he makes the workers dance
and claws the files

        the men
        their work
        to tatters

he's Narasimha the Man-lion

when wishes for undercover bribes
sprout up
and moulder
spore by spore
in a heart full of cobwebs
                    he's the Dwarf

when he roots out
people he doesn't like
as he bears his hoe-weapon
in his bent heart
                    he's Rama-with-the-axe

when he takes
loud oaths
of monogamy
in bed
and says
                Dear
                I'll never touch
                anyone else
                in this life
                not even in my heart
                    he's Lord Rama

when he hides himself
behind dark glasses
enjoying women
fore and aft
on buses and off
and takes special pleasure
in two separate houses
in faraway places
                    he's Lord Krishna

and so on and so forth
if you look more deeply
inside this man
you will see

even a thousand avatars there
              stand aside:
              he's no less than
              an avatar himself

Translated from the Tamil by Martha Ann Selby and K. Paramasivam

An Evening with Bhookh Kumari[*]

I was out on my favourite road for my evening stroll. My pace was slow, my mind sad. I was taking long breaths in order to empty my mind and smiling ruefully at my failure. One long strip of the sky was smeared with a pale redness that was fading fast, like my smile. The evening had not let her hair down yet. The road lay spread before me like a crushed cobra. I was trampling it and my self like a homeless old man. I had not yet reached the spot where I sit on a boulder and peer down at the shanties glimmering far below, my imagination hovering around them like a pigeon with broken wings. Every evening, I feel like standing on that boulder and taking a plunge into that net of coruscating shanties. I have never done it. The impulse does not strike me with horror. It is one of my many stillborn impulses.

I rarely go beyond that boulder on my evening strolls. Every old idler has a tree or a ditch, a turn or a boulder, or some such spot beyond which he does not normally stray, but beyond which he always wants to go. That evening, however, I saw someone else sitting on my boulder, and I strayed beyond it because I did not want to sit with that person. Had I noticed the intruder in time, I might have turned around. But I was slouching along with my

---

* *Bhookh* is the Hindi word for hunger; *Kumari* is the Hindi word for a virgin, a princess, a little girl, goddess Durga or Parvati. *Kumari* is a common suffix for many female names. *Bhookh Kumari* could be rendered as 'Miss Hunger' or 'Hunger Princess' in English but I have preferred to retain the name in Hindi for its sound as well as the pun and irony it lends itself to when the narrator mistakes *Bhookh Kumari* as *Bhookh Ki Mari*, which means 'a poor girl afflicted with hunger!'

head down, and it was only after I had reached the boulder that I realized my place on it had been taken. Turning around abruptly did not seem right to me. Looking straight at the little figure also did not seem right. A relentless censor is always lurking in my mind, telling me what is not right. Every evening I try in vain to throw it out of my mind. That evening I tried again. I stopped short near the boulder, then moved on, quickening my pace. I intended to look back a little later in order to be sure that I had not imagined the figure on the boulder. If it were still there, I would pretend I had just thought of an important reason to turn around and rush homeward. But I had barely gone beyond the boulder when everything began to assume another aspect. The idea of looking back got lost somewhere. I started walking briskly, breathing freely. I felt suddenly more alert, more alive. I stopped tramping on. A smile bloomed on my lips. It seemed that by going beyond the boulder, I had entered another sphere. I was astonished at the change in my mood. I started walking with my chest thrown out, my arms swaying in long sweeps, like a retired army officer or a resolute Arya Samajist. My posture is usually quite good, better than age and appearance would suggest. I tame it deliberately during my evening stroll because of my desire to descend into what I call my interior space and to empty my mind. It is a different matter that instead of achieving that descent, I begin to trample myself.

The new mood, however, did not last very long. Suddenly, I was seized by the fear that someone was following me. I know this fear. It often seizes me, especially on deserted roads, in the evening, when the day is about to breathe its last. My blood freezes and my ears turn red. I want to turn around and look but do not dare. Generally this fear leaves me after a while. It is like an epileptic fit—unpredictable and awful. As long as I am in its grip, I tense with the apprehension that it will pounce upon me any second and finish me off. It has not happened so far, but I cannot say that it never will. That evening, my body was ready for a fatal assault from behind. I could hear my pursuer's footsteps grow louder. My desire to turn around and look was killed by my old dread that if I saw no one behind me, I would go mad. At first I thought I might be hearing my own footsteps, but I knew I was not. So I waited for

193

an end to my apprehension, however unpredictable. Whenever I get soaking wet with perspiration, the pursuing footsteps fade out, and I realize my fit is about to end. But that evening I remained dry even as the shuffling sound drew close, as if someone were on my heels. Just as I thought the phantom had caught me, I heard an impish voice— 'Please turn around, I'm tired.'

It was the voice of a very young girl. I was not startled. It reassured me instead. The sound of mischief in it was sweet to my ears. My fear vanished. I stopped. She also stopped. For a few seconds I stood with my back toward her, hoping that she would step forward and speak. When she did neither, I knew that she was waiting for me, adamantly. She seemed to be a person of principles, in spite of her raw youth. I rather liked that.

She was barefoot and bareheaded. And she was smiling. She had on a dirty blue dress that barely reached her bruised knees. In her tangled unwashed hair she wore a red ribbon. Her smile, too, was red but her lips were parched, her cheeks streaked with dirt. Her hands were interlocked behind her head as she swayed on her bare feet. Her wrists were thin, her big eyes bright. It is because of the brightness in her eyes, I thought, I can see her so clearly in the dark. All my fears disappeared.

'Who are you?' I asked her tenderly.

She said her name, and I was amused, surprised, pained.

'Bhookh Ki Mari? What kind of a name is that?'

The girl laughed.

'Bhookh Ki Mari! Is that what you heard? Wonderful!'

I realized I had made a mistake. I started laughing with her. I heard the evening laughing in her laughter; she must have heard the night laughing in mine.

'It's not Bhookh Ki Mari,' she corrected me, 'it is Bhookh Kumari.'

My laughter halted. I began to brood. I did not quite know why I was brooding. Keeping quiet, however, did not seem quite right to me.

'Your name is unusual,' I said.

'But my form is not,' she rejoined.

I was impressed. A smart girl! But she shouldn't be out so late in the evening, and so far from town. I shall walk her back home.

'Yes, your form is not,' I pretended to agree with her.

'I know all about you,' she said, 'where you live, what you . . .'

'Really?' I interrupted her.

'By God!' she said in English.

I was amused but also a bit alarmed. I brushed aside the alarm and said: 'What are you doing here so late in the evening?'

'Talking to you,' she laughed.

This time her laughter irritated me. I suddenly felt my age. This brat is making fun of me! I looked at her severely and asked in a severe tone: 'Where do you live?'

'Down there, in that shanty town,' she said.

'So what are you doing up here so late in the evening?'

I had expected her to irritate me by repeating her earlier answer, but she did not.

'I came up for a stroll,' she said, 'and I wanted to see you.'

I told myself to keep cool and get rid of her by giving her some change.

'What do you want from me?' I asked.

'Nothing,' she said.

I noticed we were walking side by side now, almost like father and daughter. The thought softened me. My boulder was free now. If this girl had not followed me, I would've gone very far today and returned home very late. I felt as if she had been sent after me to keep me from going too far. I felt like telling her to rush back to her shanty town and let me resume my long walk. But I didn't really want to continue. My mood had changed. We were close to the boulder now. I stopped. She stopped too.

'What exactly were you doing here?' I asked tenderly.

'I was waiting for you,' she answered readily. 'I wanted to tell you something.'

'Why don't you, then?'

'I'll do that if you sit down with me on that boulder,' she said.

The moment I sat down on that boulder with her, I felt like taking a plunge into that net of shanties glimmering far below. She sat right in front of me, reading me with her big luminous eyes. I hope she is not crazy. Bhookh Kumari! She must have given this name to herself. Her name gave me a salty sort of amusement. Her looks too. Her voice is like that of a princess in Indian movies. I'm sure she watches a lot of movies on TV. Every shanty has a colour TV and a VCR. And a refrigerator. I checked myself. I am being uncharitable. Perhaps she sings as she begs. No I can't imagine her begging.

Her knees were bruised. Her neck was thin enough for a child's hand to encircle it. The luminosity of her eyes could be due to hunger. I felt like caressing her head, straightening the ribbon in her hair, and asking her when she had eaten last. She was gazing at me.

'Do you watch TV?' I asked her.

'Sometimes.'

'Do you have one at home?'

'No.'

My question suddenly seemed vulgar to me—like the questions some writers put in the mouths of characters who go to a brothel only to talk to prostitutes. I decided I wouldn't ask her anything. I was curious about what she wanted to tell me. How does she know all about me? Does she know the problems I am facing these days? Poor dear Bhookh Kumari! Maybe she is a fairy from somewhere. I never saw a fairy, even in my childhood. I won't see one now in my old age.

The evening had finally let her hair down. The sky was riddled with innumerable twinkling holes. The pale redness had faded out of the sky. I could hear the darkness vibrating. I sat there on that boulder like a lost old king listening to the tales of the woodcutter's little daughter. The glow in Bhookh Kumari's eyes was undiminished. Her bare feet looked like two birds fast asleep.

'Say something, Bhookh Kumari,' I said.

'I'm waiting for the darkness to thicken; you can't be in a hurry to go back home, you are alone these days, aren't you?'

This shook me up a bit. She's quite a spy.

'True, but I have to get back all the same,' I said. I felt like withdrawing my limp sentence. I also felt ashamed of myself for being so homebound.

'It's a little early for your evening ritual,' she said.

Perhaps she knows the woman who cleans for me, I thought. All of a sudden I had an intense desire to accompany her to her shanty town. But I decided not to tell her about it. That might scare

196

her away. Besides, what would I do there? I can imagine everything—filth and all. My own place is surrounded by heaps of filth. Our country is great in this respect. You are not too far from filth, no matter where you live—in the so-called posh areas or shanty towns.

'Yes, it's a little early for my evening addiction,' I said, 'but I do skip it for a day or so every now and then.'

'Really!' she said.

'By God!' I said in English.

We laughed together.

'Your laughter is nice,' she said after a short pause.

I wasn't prepared for this compliment. I couldn't tell what was in her mind. Perhaps I should have said something but I didn't.

'So you sit here on this boulder every evening and look down at the shanties glimmering far below,' she said.

I waited for her to add that she knew I thought of taking the plunge into that net of glimmering shanties but she didn't add anything.

'Can you see this boulder from your shanty?' I asked her.

There was a long pause before she opened her mouth. When she did, her voice was full of mischief—'I can see the whole world from my shanty.'

I don't know why I was shaken on hearing this. I guess I was not prepared for the flight of her fancy.

'But why didn't you stop here today?' she asked.

'Because my place was not vacant,' I said.

'So you saw me,' she asked.

'I didn't see you, but I saw that my place was occupied,' I answered.

'But it wasn't,' she said. 'I was sitting where I am sitting now, and this is not your place.'

'I consider the whole boulder as my place,' I rejoined. I had thought she would either laugh or say something to make me laugh, but she seemed lost in some other thought.

That was the first time I sat on that boulder with a smart little stranger. What is it that she wants to tell me? Why is she hesitating? I should make it easy for her, say something to draw her out. Perhaps someone in her family is sick. She needs my help. Perhaps she is just a clever little crook. I smelled meanness in my speculations and said by way of diverting my attention—'Do you go to school?'

'I used to, but not any more,' she said.

'Why did you stop?'

'I didn't like it there.'

'But why?'

'I already knew what they wanted to teach me; I'm pretty sharp,' she said with such a straight face that I couldn't help laughing. She did not laugh with me.

'Don't you believe?' she asked.

So she was aware of even this flaw in my character! I got a hold of myself and said—'Don't I believe in what?'

I was afraid she'd retort: 'In anything?' But she spared me that and said: 'In my sharpness?'

'Of course, I do . . .'

She interrupted me and said—'But you are surprised?'

The effect she had produced on me was not surprise but I had no desire to argue with her. So I kept quiet. I wanted to invite her to come and see me every evening on the same spot. I didn't do it. Somehow it didn't seem right. I was afraid of scaring her away. I was afraid she would say something that would turn me off. I made up my mind to talk less and listen more, for any wrong move or word could very well destroy the fragile harmony between us. Excessive caution would, on the other hand, affect my own tenuous spontaneity. I was in a fix—but she sat pretty in front of me, like a princess. Bhookh Kumari! I was sure her parents had little to do with that name. I thought of asking her about her parents, but then the enquiry seemed improper. The darkness had thickened by now. A thick fingernail of moon adorned the sky. Bhookh Kumari's big eyes had become even more luminous. Only undernourished children have such huge eyes. Her wrists seemed to be made of black glass but her feet were like two healthy birds.

I was disturbed in my reverie by her questions: 'The story you are struggling with these days . . . how's that going?'

'Not well,' I answered noncommittally. Perhaps she was about to tell me what she wanted to.

'I know,' she said.

'What!' I exclaimed.

'That your story is not going well.'

'But how do you know that?' I wondered.

'I'm a rag-picker, you see; I work the rubbish heaps, and the one at the back of your bungalow is in my beat,' she informed me.

I was overwhelmed.

'So apart from knowing how your story is going, I also know how you yourself are,' she told me.

'How's that?' I asked in a feeble voice.

'From the empty bottles you throw away,' she answered.

I laughed nervously, like a person overwhelmed by a prodigy. For a while my laughter disturbed the thick darkness, then it died.

'So then how am I doing these days?' I asked her.

'Not well at all; in fact, you are stuck, which is why I've come to see you,' she said blithely.

'But why here? Why didn't you drop in and see me at my bungalow; I'm always in, as you probably know,' I said.

'I do, but if I'd sought you there, you might have taken me for a beggar; you wouldn't have talked to me properly; you wouldn't have offered me a seat; you'd have considered me filthy; you'd have suspected my motives; but here in the dark we sit face to face on this boulder like two equals; of course, I'm so much younger than you—almost like one of your daughters, or even granddaughters—but here you can't intimidate me. And besides, over there, your tailless dog Gogo would've made it impossible for us to talk. He goes wild, as you don't know, as soon as he sniffs me out; I can't do my picking in peace when he is around; he guards your shredded waste paper, like a lion; I can get at it only at night . . .'

She was talking about rag-picking and rubbish heaps and Gogo but it seemed to me as if she was telling me fairy-tales. I wanted to lie down on that boulder and close my eyes and ask her to go on and on about rubbish heaps. I wondered why I had never spotted her on the rubbish heap at the back of my bungalow. I walk by that heap at least twice a day, glancing at the rag-pickers, pulling Gogo, ordering him to calm down, smelling the filth, prodding my blocked story. When Gogo pushes the back-door open and runs out of the house, I run after him, thinking that people in the lane would be wondering at my energy and my crazy fondness for Gogo. Every time I see that rubbish heap, I think of it as a heap of discarded reality. Bhookh Kumari must have seen me many times. I too must have seen her, but then why didn't I recognize her here? How could I not notice a girl like her—a red ribbon in her hair, a glow in her big eyes, and the bearing of a princess of the rubbish heaps! I felt ashamed and angry at my lack of perception. I wanted to apologize to her.

'You see,' she went on, 'I could've talked to you about these things only in the dark, here, looking at you while you are looking at those shanties far below and playing with the idea of taking a plunge . . .'

She would have gone on but I interrupted her with an indescribable exclamation. It must have struck Bhookh Kumari as ridiculous, since she burst out laughing.

'Why are you so incredulous?' she asked. 'Can't I guess what you think as you sit brooding on this boulder? I told you I am very sharp. I have imagination. True, you are a writer and I'm not, but that doesn't mean I can't imagine; you see, I too have often thought of taking the plunge that you think about. It may well be that there's something in this boulder or perhaps those shanties that tempts one to take a plunge . . .'

I gazed at her in silence. She is really marvellous. She does know everything about me. I could detect that she was parodying my train of thought and tone of speech. And she a rag-picker! Bhookh Kumari! Her big eyes glittered like stars in the dark. I wanted to touch those eyes. By now I was convinced she wouldn't be scared by anything I said or did. I was convinced she was extraordinary. The extraordinary is not confined to any one class. Or perhaps she was a fairy princess after all. She had unsettled me.

'Are you a rag-picker, really?' I asked her.

'Of course I am. What else can I be? I'm poor and uneducated. I'm lucky I belong to a family of rag-pickers. I could've been named Ghoora Bai also. My mother had that name. Rag-picking is foul work but it isn't difficult. Besides, I'm quite an expert rag-picker; I may well be the best in the city. I can tell at a glance what is worth picking and what is not. Of course, I don't pick rags only. Unlike others of my trade, I don't have to thrash about in the rubbish with my hands and feet. And then sometimes I find such wonderful things. Our shanty is a little museum of wonderful things. I've never been short of toys. Nor of clothes. Nor of food, in fact. The things people throw away! I picked this dress and this ribbon from your rubbish heap. Don't stare at my feet; I keep them bare by choice. I have a fairly large assortment of shoes but don't see any fun in wandering about unless my feet are occasionally quickened by a thorn or a pebble. People have acquired heaps of black money; that's why the rubbish heaps are rich. My mother used to bless the corporation for not removing rubbish regularly. My mother collected quite a dowry for me, entirely from the rubbish heaps. You see, we rag-pickers have a world of our own. You need not pity us. People have made millions out of us rag-pickers. Well, I look upon my work as a form of art. You write, I pick rubbish heaps. The very thought makes my mouth salivate. I can see you are feeling sick.'

I wasn't feeling sick but I *was* on the verge of tears. I wanted to stop her mouth with my hand. An extraordinary girl like her has to eat people's garbage! I was on the verge of tears born of shame and rage and impotence. I was overwhelmed by the utter obscenity of my writing and my way of life. But I couldn't lose sight of the fact that I wouldn't be able to do a thing for that fairy princess of a little girl. I wanted to get up and run off to my bungalow.

Bhookh Kumari must have seen through my dilemma, for she said: 'Well, I told you all this because you expected me to; perhaps I've told you far too much; but you should be tough; you are a writer, and a writer should have a strong stomach; he should be able to take in everything. Moreover, you have that great rubbish heap at the back of your bungalow where you must have seen filth of every kind. I'm sure you have seen me there too; I see you all the time, running after your Gogo or standing over that bent old woman eating garbage or ogling that beautiful tribal woman. You should be proud of your rubbish heap; it is full of delightful surprises, the best of them being your waste paper—crumpled into balls; I take them home and have fun unravelling them and piecing them together; some of them are totally blank; others are untorn; I like those best, for I can smooth them out and read what you have written; quite often it is the same sentence repeated several times;

I find it very funny; sometimes it is nothing more than nonsensical combinations of letters or words. Now you know how I know that neither you nor your story is doing well these days. Your working title for your story seems to be *Hunger*, hmm?'

I didn't give myself time to feel surprised or pleased at the care she took to collect my crumpled and shredded waste paper; I just let myself go, without censoring what came to my lips.

'I don't believe you are a rag-picker,' I blurted out; 'I don't believe you live in that shanty colony; I don't believe you eat garbage; I don't believe you collect my waste paper and piece or paste it together in order to read what I write; I don't believe you are sitting there in front of me; your language, your style, your sharpness, your irony, your manners, your voice, your self-confidence, your laughter, your eyes—where would a poor rag-picking girl pick all this? From rubbish heaps? From that shanty colony? From a family of rag-pickers? From my waste paper? I don't believe it. Tell me the truth. Who are you?'

I was trembling; so was my voice. Till then I had taken everything as a sort of joke. No, not as a joke but as something essentially plausible. No, not even that but something I could still take with a compound of curiosity and scepticism and amusement. But her casual talk of eating garbage and collecting my waste paper had thrown me off balance.

She took my hands in hers. My trembling soft hands seemed to be panting like two wounded birds in her stable coarse ones.

'Hey! You shouldn't go on like this,' she admonished me. 'If you can't believe, you can't; but don't take it personally; why be so emotional! You are a man of experience, a writer; you have travelled all over the world, seen all sorts of strange people; you must have seen all sorts of marvels in your dreams, if not in real life. Nothing should throw you off balance. Don't believe anything, but don't fly into this state of fury over me, poor me, poor Bhookh Kumari! All right, you are free to call me Bhookh Ki Mari! Come on, now, let's have a smile. Take a long breath. Once more. There! You are not trembling any more. An artist ought to be a magician. He should make marvels, not disbelieve them. I know you are alone these days; and you are working too hard; and you are not eating well; and you are drinking too much; and on top of it you have writer's block; I can well imagine your frustration, but I can help you; in fact, I am here this evening only to do that, you see . . .'

She went on in that vein for quite some time while I regretted my outburst quietly. Her words had a magical effect on me, though; so did the gentle pressure of her hands. I felt she was trying to dispel my disbelief with her magic. I was drawing strength from her words and hands. I had a great desire to ask her to join me in taking a plunge into that net of glimmering shanties far below. I was regaining my composure gradually but my essential disbelief was still unshaken. I told myself I had no right to shout at the poor dear stranger. I told myself to relax and hear what she was saying, instead of resisting it. Soon enough I was my normal, sane self.

'I shouldn't have lost control,' I said.

'Never mind,' she said.

She let go of my hands. The beautiful coarseness of her small hands smoothed my big flabby hands. Neither of us spoke for a while. I kept peering into her big bright eyes, she into my small dim ones.

'But don't you believe?' she asked finally.

I wasn't prepared for that question. Earlier when she had raised the same question, out of consideration for me, she had given it a narrow meaning; this time she had left it wide open. An answer to that question would have involved me in an examination of my entire life. So I kept quiet. She did not press her question.

'How old are you?' I asked, primarily to take my attention away from the thought that I might have extinguished the magic of the evening by my disbelief.

'About twelve or thirteen, and you?'

'About sixty or sixty-one,' I said.

'You can walk like a sixteen-year-old when you want to,' she remarked.

I smiled even as I felt flattered. So she even knows my sensitivity about my age.

'Now, if you promise,' she went on, 'not to fly into a rage, I'll say what I want to.'

'I promise,' I said solemnly.

'Tell me, then, why that story of yours, *Hunger*, is causing you so much difficulty; why doesn't it move?' She looked very concerned as she said this.

I wasn't prepared for her question. I thought of saying that every story had always caused me difficulty, that difficulty was the price one paid for the delight of finishing a story, that every artist had his problems, and other such rot. But I couldn't possibly do that to her, to Bhookh Kumari. So I said: 'I don't know why; I don't want to talk about it either; I'm afraid I'll kill the desire to write that story if I do, and then you won't find those crumpled balls of waste paper on that heap.'

'Don't talk about it then,' she said, 'for I've got addicted to smoothing those crumpled balls of paper and putting them together into readable stuff; I've a whole heap of them in my shanty; my mother would've burnt them.'

'What happened to your mother?'

'She died.'

'Of what?'

'Of cholera.'

I didn't have the heart to ask her about her father. But she seemed to have divined my curiosity.

'I don't have a father,' she went on, 'I mean I don't know who he was or is; my mother never told me about him; people of my colony called me a bastard; I used to swear and throw stones at them, which made them torture me even more. Lately, I've stopped minding them. One night my mother came to me in a dream and advised me not to mind. It was good advice, for people have stopped torturing me now. It doesn't give them any pleasure any more to call me a bastard since I've stopped flaring up and hitting back. People would do anything for pleasure.'

Her last sentence was full of the wisdom of the world.

'I too am fond of writing,' she told me cheerfully.

I wasn't surprised but I kept quiet.

'You must be thinking, "Who isn't"?' she said.

I wasn't thinking that. I couldn't tell what I was thinking about. In order to get out of the darkness of my thoughts I said: 'What do you write?'

'Nothing. I'm just fond of it. For now I'm just busy collecting paper and experience.'

204

Her experience shone like a magical glow-worm in the darkness of my thoughts. I brightened up a little. I told myself I'd take her home with me for dinner. I'd ask her to wash her hands first, I might even ask her to take a quick bath, I'd give her a shirt and a pair of trousers and have her old clothes thrown on the heap, I'd let her keep the red ribbon; she would emerge like a flower from under her dirt; perhaps I'd have her admitted into a good school ...

I'd strayed far in my fantasy and was a little embarrassed by its romantic colour. I feared that Bhookh Kumari would hear my thoughts and say: 'What a wild imagination?' But instead she said in a mysteriously mature voice: 'You won't believe, but I can really help you out of your block.'

I gave a start. My fantasy disappeared. Bhookh Kumari was waiting for my response to her offer of help.

'Forget about my disbelief; I accept your offer of help,' I said.

Bhookh Kumari got up and stood erect on the boulder. She straightened her blue dress, yawned, and said with a smile: 'Well, then, you'll have to come over to my shanty and stay with me for a few days; of course, you'll have to take off your fancy clothes and wear rags; you'll sleep by the side of an open drain and put your bungalow and bathrooms out of mind; you'll have to go back to the days of your youth when you knew hunger and dreamt of abolishing it, you'll have to eat the garbage of other people; you'll have to overcome your nausea . . .'

She went on like that for a while longer as I listened to her intently, my head down like that of a devotee. Her voice seemed to be descending from heaven. I couldn't get up the nerve to say that her conditions were acceptable to me.

Then she stopped her outpour abruptly. I raised my head. She smiled. She had seen through my hesitation.

'You don't have to decide right now,' she said, 'I shall come to you in your dreams one of these nights. Till then you should let my conditions sink into your mind.'

She jumped off the boulder and ran down the slope toward her home glimmering far below. I sat there for a while, looking at her receding figure, then got up and walked wearily back to my bungalow.

Many days have gone by. Every night I wait for the dream in

which Bhookh Kumari will appear to me again and I give her my
answer.

Translated from the Hindi by the author

Note on Contributors

Chandra Agrawal teaches English at Morgan State University. Previously, she has taught at the University of Michigan and Mercy College of Detroit. Her publications include *Studies in Indian Literature and Culture* (Lucknow, 1977) and *Jaya Shankar Prasad*, a special issue of the *Journal of South Asian Literature*.

Meena Alexander lives in Manhattan and teaches in the writing program at Columbia University. Her novel *Nampally Road* was published in 1991. Her long poem *Night-Scene, the Garden* (Red Dust) and her memoir *Fault Lines* (Feminist Press) were published in Spring 1992.

Agha Shahid Ali, a poet from Kashmir, teaches English and creative writing at Hamilton College. His collections of poetry include *Bone-Sculpture* (Writers Workshop), *The Half-inch Himalayas* (Wesleyan), *A Walk Through the Yellow Pages* (SUN/gemini Press), and *A Nostalgist's Map of America* (Norton). He is also the translator of *The Rebel's Silhouette* by the Urdu poet Faiz Ahmed Faiz. He published *The Belovéd Witness* (a selection from his five books of poetry) with Penguin India in 1992.

Ambai, *nom de plume* of C. S. Lakshmi, is a historian now working on women's histories of South India. She is the author of two volumes of short stories, and of the critical study, *The Face Behind the Mask: Women in Tamil Literature*. She was a Homi Bhaba Fellow for 1990–92 and lives in Bombay.

Paramita Banerjee is pursuing her doctorate in social philosophy at Jadavpur University. She has published articles on theatre and women's issues, as well as poetry, in a number of literary

Crow

there
a plain
countless crows on the plain
          could be stones
if they flew then certainly crows

white
sky
countless stones in the sky
          could be crows
if they fall then certainly stones

a
crow
countless skies in the crow
          could be plains
if they heave then certainly skies

a
stone
countless plains in the stones
          could be skies

if plains then certainly stones
if skies then certainly crows

Translated from the Gujarati by Karamshi Pir

A. K. Ramanujan

Elegy

a grown son's tears in a restaurant mix their salt
with a colleague's long-awaited sudden
death in Jodhpur

the breath of garlic as we enter
the elevator suffocates me
for this colleague

chewed on twelve garlic cloves every morning
as a cure for cancer after
an amputation

quoted Keats on the sparrow in the sun
the grape pressed into his palate
believed in homœopathic

doses of cowdung Shelley's chemical
experiments and the calcium deficiency
of his high-pitched verse

how native doctors had little white pills
for homesickness abroad how they
diagnosed your liver

and kidney by seeing whether your urine
stream was one or divided
in two did you know

it was not Wordsworth but his sister
who heard the solitary reaper
by which time

the elevator had reached the eighteenth floor
and I'd to get out and sign a health
insurance form

unable to shake off the whiff of garlic or
the taste of the grape now round
now crushed

in the mouth of Keats in the mouth
of my friend who had mixed them
into my breath

Butcher's Tao

The butcher in China
looks long at a bull till he sees
the bull and how

the beast is jointed,
then moves his knife
in the spaces

he has learned
by heart with his hand
moving on the bull

and the bull
is now sirloin,

tenderloin, prime rib,
dogbone, two horns

for weddings or combs,
sandals for the pedestrian

peasant, saddle and rein
for horse, thong and head

for kettledrums to scare away
eclipses from the sun,

ghosts from processions,
or summon cities

to banquets, friends and
enemies to battle,

the blood in the bucket
ready for sprinkling

on children with polio
and village borders.

The rest is batter
for blood puddings.

The Tryst

When the whole city is asleep
I take off my anklets
and come into your room
on soft, stolen steps.

You lie there, unmoving,
on the disordered bed,
books strewn all around.
In their midst, alone, you lie asleep,
a smile of some strange contentment
on your sleeping face.
I sit quietly by the bed,
smooth your dishevelled hair,
then, bend down and with my sharp nails
tear open your chest,
and with both my hands scoop out
a fistful of pulsating soft pink flesh.

I am spellbound by the odor of that flesh
I hold it to my breast.
For a moment,
the word and the silence become one,
then, sky and earth—
they become one.

Before you wake
I put it back in place,
caress your open chest.
The wound fills up in a moment
as if nothing had happened.

As before, you go on sleeping
I walk, quietly, from your room.

Translated from the Oriya by Jagannath Prasad Das and Arlene Zide

213

Vinda Karandikar

Himayoga
A Meditation on Snow; Chicago, 1967-68

I. THE MAYFLOWER PILGRIMS

When the pilgrims dawned on the shore with their own skin
    for a charter,
The sun dipped behind a cloud. The pelicans tidied up their
    white
Ankle-length gowns. The leafless trees, unnamed as yet,
    whispered inquisitively
Among themselves. Only the fearless snow understood the
    situation.
For only the snow had borne the burning touch of the
    visitors' soles, had read the fate
Inscribed in their cracks. When the pilgrims dawned on the
    shore, it was time for the tide
To recede, but the water lingered for a while. The pilgrims
    understood.
They placed a nickel of leftover memories on its palm, as a
    tip for the ocean.

Then slowly they settled down to the work ahead, with
    puritanical determination.
one mingled with the pelicans to sprout wings; another
    merged with the trees
To grow rooted in the soil; the third one cried out
    prophetically,

'Tattered sails end up as cloth for underwear and flags';
    the fifth one picked
Sixteen hundred and twenty lice from the sixth one's hair.
    But before their work began,
The strong ones gathered wood, and lit fires—from which
    arose the incandescent suns

II. AFTER CROSSING THE ATLANTIC

I had no notion that if the shadows of these leafless trees
Even touched my body, it would sprout the leaves of the
    jackfruit tree;
No notion that this biting wind would bring me news of the
    mango blossom;
That the snow here would make the secular world bear fruit,
And impregnate the Golden Womb that lies beyond the Sutlej.
I had no notion that having crossed four thousand miles of
    ocean, in the end,
I would arrive only in my own country; that the Ganga would
    be flowing through the Mississippi;
That the Ganga's arms would hold Arsenal Island in their
    embrace.

How hard it is to arrive in another country without giving
    up one's own!
For a moment in Janeseo, outside Father Dagley's house,
    I thought I saw
A bush of holy basil growing in a flowerpot; at the lively
    dance at night,
I saw many cowherd-girls and many Krishnas moving in sweet
    harmony;
I came out of my daydream with a start, embarrassed. How
    hard it is to reach another country.
The path that leads from one's doorstep to Mathura has no
    end, even when one has crossed the Atlantic.

At a striptease show, every rag becomes a Draupadi; these trees
      bare themselves with the same gravity,
Discarding their leaves in September. And now on December's
      branch,
A last leftover hymn-like leaf, lighting up the incense of its
      renunciation.
Now all the trees have won their battle with death; they've lost
      the green signs of their names;
They're moving towards the sublime by the way of the dreary;
    they
      pose a riddle;
Inverted brooms that scrape the sky. Icy winds, sharp as an axe,
      begin to blow and sing,
Churning up the rhythms of jazz in the great primordial breath:
      aum, rhaum, rheem, rhoom . . .

Even as it renounces the world, nature needs the luxury of ritual
In this land of plenty. But a touch of this snow brought me back
      to my senses.
Today, even in the first cold spell, I felt that my clothes
      were a burden;
And when I removed their weight, my skin beneath the layers
    sensed
Their kinship with cotton. Someone arrived from the north
      with full-blown sails;
Began to call out the summons of the ice; 'Present, sir,' I cried,
      coming awake.
When the naked body has encountered the snow, it sparks off
      a different fire.

IV. SNOW IN HYDE PARK

These children are the true descendants of the abominable
      snowman!

Pelting each other with snow; boisterous in the snow;
     snowballed by snow;
Snoweyes, snowlimbs, snowmad; more snowy than snow.
Sssnow . . . sssnow . . . the skeletons of trees crazed
     with snow,
Fired by this dance, the Shake; doing a deathdance as
     the blizzard thickens,
Emerging from their coffins and dancing on the boards like
     a bunch of demons.

Sssnoo. Sssnoo. Sssnoo on the steps of the exhausted church.
     Virgin sssnoo
Freezing in the cold. Ancient sssnoo on the bald pates
     of buildings.
Sssnoo rotten and mashed on the muddy road. Sssnoo. Sssnoo.

Snow again. A pair of footprints dripping through the snow,
     some lonely creature
Coming apart at the seams. The fairy-tale of snow in that mind.
     A fairy-anguish, gushing,
Skating on ice and snow. Snow that glows. Its cold brand
     on the tongue.

A snow-yoga in reverse. A meditation that stops time on the
verge
     of speed. One that makes
Henry Moore's *Nuclear Energy* an image of elephant-headed
Ganesh,
     to threaten all dualities.

V. PILGRIM AND LINEAGE

My children, my children's children, their children, then again
     those children's children,
Children stemming from children like this until, one endless day,
The whole root with its gnarl of offshoots will wither
     away . . .

217

That moment, present although far, travels towards me across
      the snow's endlessness;
Its shadow arrives ahead of it, reaching my feet with the ease
      of the snake
Who crawls through a jujube tree; a shadow that sinks its fangs
Into every act of Vishnu's Ten Avatars on their genealogical
      pilgrimage,
And makes the chanting of spells meaningless. I see the Third
Eye
      of the Formless One
Intent on the end of everything; what I see is only the white
      of His eye, as perishable as snow.
Those who have seen the pupil of that eye, the image in that
pupil,
      the eye of that image,
The eye in the eye, the eye . . . aiye . . . eaye . . .
      whom . . . who . . .
My roots, the roots of my roots, then their roots, the root
      at the root of all roots;
Perhaps even those roots don't know when and where that root
      took root.
Only the snow has the passport to visit all the sacred places
      on the pilgrim's genealogical route.

VI. MEMORIES OF HOME

Memories of home. The bolt on the door, fastened, unfastened.
The familiar smell of the bath-soap. Those four people, their
      breaths.
A pair of shorts, its drawstring missing. A mouthful of
      star-fruit.
A crow in the eaves. A broken thermometer, a knot finally
      undone.
Quarrelling violently. Polishing rice in the mortar in a
      neighbour's kitchen.
Losing a button; finding it; then losing it again. The children's
      homework, beta and theta.

Tying up the broom when it falls apart. Cementing a cracked
    windowpane.
A tangy homemade soup, the sting of salt in a pickle. The
Goddess
    Gauri and Lord Ganesh.
An oilstain on the mirror. Anger and sulking. 'We're-always-
    in-your-way . . .'
'All lies, lies,' etcetera. 'Can-you-see-the-talcum-powder-
    anywhere,' etcetera.
Removing a jammed cork successfully. Too much food served
    on the plate. Expectations, disappointments.
Losing a bargain with a buyer of empty bottles and cans.
    The bathroom, occupied.
A ball lost forever. Picking wax from my ear while standing
    at the window.
The angle of destiny, like a ray of sunlight, in calm, deep
    water. Her strength, who's now alone.

VII. ON THE LAKE SHORE

Three men went past talking among themselves, one squeezed
    another's hand,
The third one reared with laughter like a horse neighing . . . .
Just because he neighed, why should a flower flower on this
    dark red tree,
With its eye squinting at the south? A police car, aware
    of everything,
Steals up behind that car which went by speeding; but why
should
    its existential wail
Be cut off at precisely this moment? The moment I spotted the
    rippled shadows
Of the clouds travelling across Lake Michigan, they sensed my
    presence
And dissolved in the water. What's this conspiracy?

The same error has occurred on the typewriter for the third time,
    an O

Pushes out and takes the place of an A, as large as a gaping eye.
What's the secret of this incident? What's this conspiracy?
These mad capers may not be as mindless as they seem. What's
the
     use
Of extricating myself by saying they have nothing to do with me,
If the One who says 'I am One' changes like this in the end to
     'I am Many'?

Translated from the Marathi by Vinay Dharwadker

Vinay Dharwadker

Some Contexts of Modern Indian Poetry[*]

Like poetry produced at other times and in other places, twentieth-century poetry from India is connected in numerous, often complicated ways to the world in which it is written, read, and circulated. Unlike poetry in other national traditions, however, it appears in about twenty important languages, thirteen of which are represented in these pages. The variety of languages relates modern Indian poems to an unusually large number of contexts, many of which make individual texts significant simultaneously at the local, regional, national, and international levels. In order to understand how these contexts mediate particular poems, it is especially useful to look synoptically at three of them: the history of poetic movements in India during the first half of the twentieth century; the network of national and international allusions, references, and influences which gives modern Indian poetry its intertextual resonance; and the social circumstances in which recent Indian writers have produced their poetry.

1

One of the principal contexts of modern Indian poetry is its history, which can be explored initially as a succession of interacting poetic

---

[*] A longer version of this essay will appear as the Afterword to *Modern Indian Poetry: An Anthology*, edited by Vinay Dharwadker and A. K. Ramanujan, forthcoming from Oxford University Press in India and the University of California Press in the United States.

The essay refers to several writers included in this issue, whose names are set in boldface for ease of reference.

movements. Throughout the twentieth century, movements, counter-movements, schools, factions, and styles of poetry have appeared all over India in significant numbers and with great regularity. Some of them have been national in scope, bringing together most of the languages, while others have been local or regional in character, being confined to one or two languages and communities. Some movements have lasted for a quarter of a century or more, and have involved more than one generation of writers. Others, in contrast, have survived for less than a decade, and have been centred around small (but influential) coteries of friends.

In general, the series of successive, overlapping, and interacting nation-wide movements in poetry which appeared in the first half of the twentieth century prepared the ground for the mixture of schools and styles we find in contemporary India. The earliest of the 'national' poetic movements emerged between about 1910 and 1930, when the various languages collectively went through a phase of intensely *nationalist* writing. This movement, which had its origins in the nineteenth century, included hundreds of popular poets who wrote (or tried to write) rousing poems about Mother India, her glorious, heroic, and ancient past, her present courage in the face of British imperialism, and her idealistic determination to win her political and cultural freedom in the near future. It also included dozens of more serious poets, most of whom played prominent roles in the freedom movement, both locally and nationally. Among them were figures like Rabindranath Tagore (Bengali) and Aurobindo Ghose (English), whose work is still read widely, as well as poets like Shridhar Pathak, Maithilisharan Gupta, and Makhanlal Chaturvedi (Hindi), whose work is now read by smaller regional audiences and mainly—one hopes—for its historical interest. During the nationalist movement, Indian poetry as a whole seemed to be at one with its social and political circumstances, and the poets seemed to be equally at one with their audiences. In subsequent decades, with the 'death' of nationalism and idealism, these identifications gave way to an alienation between poets and their publics, and a disjunction between poems and their immediate situations.

Between the two world wars, and especially between about

1920 and 1935, the Indian languages passed through a new nation-wide phase of *Romantic* writing (an earlier, longer one had appeared in the nineteenth century), which overlapped with the nationalist movement. In this phase a large number of poets attempted to redo, at least in part, what the Romantics in England had done more than a century earlier. The models for these Indian poets included the better-known works of William Wordsworth, John Keats, and Percy Bysshe Shelley, the minor lyrics of Lord Byron, and the poems of lesser figures like Thomas Hood (as well as the writings of Sir Walter Scott, Lord Alfred Tennyson, and Henry Wadsworth Longfellow). This type of displaced and modified Romanticism appeared, for example, in Assamese, in the works of Lakshminath Bezbarua, Raghunath Raichoudhary, and Jatindranath Duara; in Telugu, in the Bhavakavitvam school of poetry led by Rayprolu Subbarao and Devulapalli Krishnashastry; and in Marathi, in the poetry of Balkavi and that of Madhav Julian and the poets of the Ravi Kiran Mandal (these writers are practically untranslatable now). By and large, the twentieth-century Indian Romantic movement emphasized the primacy of the unique human individual and his or her unified sensibility, concentrating on 'intense' personal experience, emotional spontaneity, lyricism, and sincerity to produce a body of writing that dealt mainly with nature, love, desire, melancholy, childhood, simplicity, nostalgia, and fine feelings. These private, often idiosyncratic explorations generally contrasted sharply with the public rhetoric of nationalist poetry, and created a distance between the poet and his or her audience and the text and its contexts. But they contributed nonetheless to the definition of a distinctive modern Indian self and even an alternative national identity, in which a poet introspectively became the site where one or more older Indian traditions manifested themselves. Of the writers included in this issue, **Mahadevi Varma** (Hindi) is the only one who began as a Romantic, publishing her famous and influential early poems in the 1920s and 1930s, and acquiring a major national reputation well before the Second World War.

Two new, frequently intersecting and simultaneous national movements appeared in the 1930s to complicate the dialectic of nationalism and romanticism (most Romantics were nationalists, but many nationalists were not Romantics). One was the *Progressive* movement, launched effectively by the national conference of the Progressive Writers' Association at Lucknow in 1936, with a presidential address by Munshi Premchand, the foremost fiction writer in modern Hindi. The Progressive movement, some of whose early proponents continued to write until the 1980s, emphasized the significance of Marxist thought and socialist and communist ideals for the various Indian literatures, especially Urdu, Hindi, Bengali, Gujarati, Marathi, English, Telugu, Kannada, and Malayalam. Many of the Progressive writers criticized and rejected the matriotism and romanticism of their predecessors, and attempted to paint a bleak, often starkly violent, even 'anti-nationalistic' portrait of Indian society, choosing invective, satire, and irony over epic seriousness and lyricism. Among the poets in these pages, **Raghuvir Sahay, Kedarnath Singh** (both Hindi), **Vinda Karandikar** (Marathi), and **Sunil Gangopadhyay** (Bengali) are prominent examples of writers influenced by the Progressive movement.

The other nation-wide movement that started in the 1930s—and continued to affect writers and readers until the end of the 1970s—was the Indian counterpart of Anglo-American *modernism*, in which poets in practically every language broke away from traditional (often highly Sanskritized) metres, stanza patterns, styles, materials, and themes to invent 'free verse' poetry. In exploring new forms of writing, these poets often took up distinctively high modernist positions (for example, in Marathi, B.S. Mardhekar in the 1940s), or combined them with Progressive existentialist perspectives in the Indian context (**Vinda Karandikar** in the 1950s), or with avant garde, especially surrealist, viewpoints (Dilip Chitre and **Arun Kolatkar** in the 1960s). Using a range of this sort, they concentrated on such themes as the disintegration of traditional communities and familiar cultural institutions, the alienation of the individual in urban society, the dissociation of thought and feeling, the disasters of modernization, the ironies of daily existence, and the anguish of unresolved doubts and anxieties. In this issue, **Kunwar Narayan** (Hindi), **Nabaneeta Dev**

Sen (Bengali), and **Gulam mohammed Sheikh** (Gujarati) are among the more distinguished writers influenced by the modernist movement in Indian letters.

In the decade immediately after independence (1947), the literatures in most of the Indian languages underwent a different kind of upheaval at approximately the same time, launching more or less 'regional' poetic movements that were often simply called *new poetry* (for instance, *nai kavita* in Hindi and *nava kavya* in Marathi). Although the various new poetry movements of the late 1940s and the 1950s were sufficiently similar to constitute a loosely integrated nation-wide phenomenon, they retained a local or regional character in keeping with the renewed regional chauvinisms that surfaced in the 1950s when independent India was divided into states along linguistic and cultural lines (Orissa became the Oriya-speaking state, Andhra Pradesh the Telugu-speaking state, and so on). By and large, the new poetry in different regions emerged as a combination or mixture of styles and concerns developed earlier by the major 'national' movements of the first half of the twentieth century. In some instances, it revived the old nationalist and Romantic attitudes to celebrate the end of the British Raj. In many other cases, however, it articulated hesitation, doubt, unease, skepticism, and even outright anger or despair over the disappointments of post-colonialism, bringing together modernist style and Progressive critique to attack the new Indian order under the leadership of Jawaharlal Nehru and the Congress Party (for example, **Vinda Karandikar** fuses Progressivism and experimental modernism in his 'high' *nava kavya* style in Marathi). In the end of the 1950s, the new poetry in languages like Hindi, Marathi, Kannada, and Bengali had begun to give way to an unprecedented social and political reconfiguration of the Indian literary world, which I shall discuss in the final sections of this essay.

2

A second major context of nineteenth- and twentieth-century Indian poetry is the variety of Indian and foreign literatures surrounding it. In the web of intertextual relationships spreading outwards from this poetry, 'foreign influences' have played a crucial role in the emergence of Indian modernity. The same is true of the older literatures of the subcontinent, which constitute the 'domestic sources' that Indian poets have constantly plundered in their quest for novelty, modernity, and meaning. Reading modern Indian poems in the context of various literatures and literary relationships helps us to explain phenomena that we cannot explain easily by analysing the history of poetic movements.

Indian sources and foreign influences play different kinds of roles, with each also serving several distinct purposes. Some *foreign* influences work at the level where an entire Western literature deeply affects one or more modern Indian literatures. English literature is an obvious case in point, since it has pervasively influenced all the Indian language traditions since the nineteenth century. Other Western literatures also enter the picture, but they work differently and differentially. For instance, poets from Bengal, whether they write in Bengali or English or both, have had a more or less unique, obsessive relationship with the French language and its literature for almost one hundred and fifty years now. 'The French Connection' first appeared in Bengal around the third quarter of the nineteenth century, in the work and careers of poets like Michael Madhusudan Dutt (Bengali and English) and Toru Dutt (English). It then resurfaced strongly just before and soon after the middle of the twentieth century in the generations represented by, say, Buddhadev Bose and **Nabaneeta Dev Sen** (both bilingual in Bengali and English), who have extensively worked out rather agonistic connections with Baudelaire, Mallarme, Rimbaud, and Valery. Some of the distinctive qualities of modern Bengali poetry—for instance, its immersion in metropolitan culture, its love-hate relationship with modernity, its simultaneous provincialism and cosmpolitanism, its zeal for revolutions—carry strong traces of French influence. The Bengali situation is intriguing because exact parallels in the other Indian languages appear only piecemeal in the work of individual poets, as when we find a strong interest in the French symbolists and twentieth-century avant garde poets in **Arun Kolatkar** and Dilip Chitre (both bilingual in Marathi and English).

The anomaly of the situation of French literature in India is heightened by its contrast with two other prominent foreign literatures. Spanish poetry from Latin America, particularly the work of Pablo Neruda (probably the single most influential poet in the world in recent times), has generated a much more evenly spread interest among poets in different Indian languages, whether Bengali and Hindi, or Gujarati, Oriya, and Malayalam. Similarly, American Beat poetry of the 1950s and 1960s has also had a widespread effect, chiefly through the influence of Allen Ginsberg, drawing strong (favourable) responses from all over the subcontinent. Neither of these bodies of writing, however, has yet affected Indian poetry as deeply as English Romantic, Victorian, and high modernist writing has, or for a comparable length of time.

In the modern Indian situation, foreign influences work not only at the level of whole literatures and movements, but also at the level of specific genres, and at that of isolated connections between individual authors. In the case of genres, between the first quarter of the nineteenth century and the third quarter of the twentieth, for example, the English and European sonnet has predictably seduced many strong and weak poets in languages like Bengali, Marathi, English, and Urdu; while in recent decades the Japanese haiku has sparked off experiments in, say, Kannada and Gujarati. It is worth observing that this mechanics of imitation, derivation, and transfer also appears in the case of modern Indian prose, where, for instance, the nineteenth-century Russian short story— Chekhov, Turgenev, Dostoevsky, Tolstoy—remained an obvious primary model for Indian writers for more than half a century.

In contrast, in the case of particular influences on individual writers, we find a much wider range of obsessions and affiliations, some of them quite startling. To mention only a few instances and selected literary relationships, among the writers represented here we find strong, self-consciously established affiliations between **B. C. Ramachandra Sharma** (Kannada) and W. B. Yeats; **Jayanta Mahapatra** (English) and John Ashbery; Dilip Chitre (Marathi) and Hart Crane; **Vinda Karandikar** (Marathi) and G. M. Hopkins and W. H. Auden; and **Kedarnath Singh** (Hindi) and Hans Magnus Enzensberger and Vasko Popa.

If the context of foreign literatures helps us to unravel lines of influence in the network of modernity, the context of *Indian literatures* allows us to separate the varieties of revival, retrieval, reworking, and renovation that revitalize the Indian poetic imagination on its home ground. Although all modern poets 'reject' the past in order to become 'modern,' they often end up using the past imaginatively and constructively in a multitude of ways: many modern writers are, quite paradoxically, traditionalists and classicists. We find modern Indian poets replicating this paradox from a variety of poetic, political, and philosophical positions. Thus, since the turn of the century, numerous poets have drawn extensively on the forms, devices, voices, and motifs of the *bhakti* (devotional) poetry produced in the Dravidian and Indo-Aryan languages during the past one thousand years or more. **Mahadevi Varma** (Hindi) and Indira Sant (Marathi), for example, have revitalized Mirabai's sixteenth-century Rajasthani poetry of love, separation, and union with a divine lover (*viraha bhakti*), combining it with nineteenth-century English Romanticism; B.S. Mardhekar and **Vinda Karandikar** have turned to the examples of Jnaneshwar (thirteenth century) and Tukaram (seventeenth century) in Marathi; and **Arun Kolatkar** has fused Jnaneshwar and Tukaram, among others, with Rimbaud, the dadaists, the surrealists, and the Beat poets. In the past two or three decades the Indian-English poets have continued to work in a similar vein: Nissim Ezekiel has used classical Sanskrit models to produce delightful experimental poster poems; Arvind Krishna Mehrotra has exploited second-century Prakrit originals to write witty, epigrammatic poems; and **R. Parthasarathy** has drawn on the Tamil classics, while **Agha Shahid Ali** has reworked the *ghazal* tradition of the last three centuries to reflect on contemporary Indian experience in exile.

The range of affiliations generated by the convergence of national and international literary contexts described above is probably best represented in contemporary Indian verse by **A. K. Ramanujan**'s equally distinguished poetry in English and Kannada. Ramanujan's bilingual work crosses numerous historical, cultural, and poetic boundaries as it resonantly brings together Cassandra and the *Mundaka Upanishad*, the Tamil *sangam* poets and the Kannada *bhakti* poets, Pascal and Yeats, Cesar Vallejo and Rene Char, reflections on pointillism, and meditations on Zen, the imagistic lyric and the satiric prose poem, the modernist monologue and the postmodernist collage. Significantly enough, Rabindranath Tagore (Bengali) and Subramania Bharati (Tamil) perfected many of these strategies on a large scale around the beginning of this century. They drew boldly on Vedic hymns, Upanishadic dialogues, Vedantic concepts, and *bhakti* poems, on Baul songs in Bengali, religious-erotic poetry in Maithili, or proverbs and riddles in Tamil, and on grandmothers' tales, nursery rhymes, lullabies, and abecedaria—even as they learned from Tennyson and Browning, Whitman and Mallarme, Eliot and Pound.

3

A third crucial context of modern Indian poetry is its varied social world, which shapes the lives of the poets, their education and literary training, their relationships with their medium and their audiences, their understanding of the conventions and functions of authorship, as well as their identities in a rapidly changing literary culture. The heterogeneity of the Indian social world permeates many different literary institutions, takes the form of synchronic variations as well as historical transformations, and surfaces at several distinct levels of analysis.

For example, heterogeneity is evident in the fact that all modern Indian writers do *not* come from the same social class. It is true that the majority of modern Indian writers consists of middle-class men and women, but the so-called middle class in India is itself a spectrum of different positions, varying by language, region, religion, caste, occupation, income, education, degree of urbanization, and so on (with its lower segments living below the line that defines 'poverty' in Europe and America). But even though this makes it possible to claim that the Indian literatures by and large are a middle-class phenomenon, it is important to remember that some Indian writers come from upper-class backgrounds (for example, Rabindranath Tagore and Sudhindranath Dutta earlier, and Arun Joshi, Salman Rushdie, and Bharati Mukherjee now), while others, in increasing numbers in recent decades, come from low-income families in large cities and small towns (for instance, G. M. Muktibodh), impoverished village communities in the countryside (Bahinabai Chaudhari, Anuradha Mahapatra), and even the bottomless bottom of the caste hierarchy (Daya Pawar, Namdeo Dhasal, Hira Bansode, Jyoti Lanjevar, Narayan Surve).

In fact, when we survey the modern Indian literatures systematically, they turn out to constitute an essentially mixed institution that draws writers as well as readers and audiences from many different parts of the Indian social world. Thus, among the best-known recent poets in the major languages—such as those represented here—we find businessmen (**Kunwar Narayan**), commercial artists (Dilip Chitre), economists (**P. S. Rege**), physicists (**Jayanta Mahapatra**), professors of language and literature (**Nabaneeta Dev Sen, Meena Alexander, Vinda Karandikar, Kedarnath Singh**), local administrators and national-level bureaucrats (**B. C. Ramachandra Sharma, Ramakanta Rath, Sitakanta Mahapatra**), social workers (**Mahadevi Varma**), journalists (**Sunil Gangopadhyay, Raghuvir Sahay**), publishers' editors (R. Parthasarathy), advertising executives (Arun Kolatkar), painters and art-teachers (**Gulam mohammed Sheikh**), and full-time writers (**Amrita Pritam**). This makes the twentieth-century Indian poetic world heterogeneous, unpredictable, and exciting when compared to the sedate or colourless academic-literary worlds we sometimes find elsewhere.

Nor do all modern Indian poets study literature formally beyond the high-school level: their education in college ranges from Sanskrit and the fine arts, to law, the natural sciences, and engineering. Most of them acquire or develop their literary tastes outside the institutional classroom, most often in local networks of writers, translators, critics, intellectuals, and "activists" of various shades and colours who meet in coffee-houses and tea-stalls, private homes and campus common-rooms, or even at cinema theatres, movie clubs, libraries, and art galleries. The liveliest and most influential modern Indian writing still comes out of these 'autonomous associations' characteristic of a 'civil society' in which writers write chiefly in order to exercise their common citizenship, both politically and apolitically, as fully as possible.

The principal medium in which modern Indian poets exercise their citizenship is, of course, the medium of print. Their work appears constantly in mass-media weeklies and monthlies, small literary magazines, institutional journals, edited anthologies, individual books, and posthumous editions of collected works. In some languages there are more than a dozen periodicals that publish poetry regularly; in others, there may be less than a handful. The languages with the ten or twelve largest populations of native speakers have large (sometimes very large) regional publishing industries, and in each of them there are several publishers who concentrate on contemporary literature. In a language like Bengali, or Hindi, or Marathi, at least a couple of hundred poets publish their work in any given year; most of them appear in magazines, but a substantial number of them also publish books, some privately, some with small presses, and others with well-known publishing houses. An established poet may sell between 2,000 and 5,000 copies of a book of poems over five years or so; a good anthology of contemporary poetry may sell out two or three such editions in a single decade. The modern classics and literary bestsellers in each language—Tagore in Bengali, Ghalib in Urdu, Deokinandan Khatri and Premchand in Hindi prose—run into forty or fifty large printings in the course of a century.

Contemporary Indian poets and their audiences, however, do not communicate only through the abstract medium of print. They come face to face at poetry readings organized by colleges, literary societies, libraries, and private cultural centres and state academies, as well as by political groups and political parties. They congregate at local, state, and national writers' conferences and at international cultural festivals. Besides, the poets now travel abroad on exchange programmes and reading circuits set up by Indian embassies and Indian immigrants' associations at the invitation of book fair committees and foreign governments. The readers and listeners they reach are equally varied and scattered: politically partisan 'mass audiences' in Belgaum and Aurangabad, small groups of writers and academics at the local Max Mueller Bhavan or the Alliance Française, fashionable women at the India International Centre, and coteries of expatriate Indians and South Asia specialists in London and Chicago.

The picture of the modern Indian poets' varied world is complicated by the fact that many of them have been and are writers and intellectuals or artists in the larger sense. Besides poems, they publish short stories, novellas, and novels, plays and literary criticism, essays on social issues and travel accounts. **Amrita Pritam**, for example, is not only the best-known contemporary woman poet in Punjabi, but also the most important modern writer in the language in general, with more than seventy collections of poems and short stories, novels, autobiographical accounts, and other kinds of works to her credit. At a more general cultural level, painter-poets like **Gulam mohammed Sheikh** and **Gieve Patel** are as central to the history of modern Gujarati poetry and Indian English poetry, respectively, as they are to the history of twentieth-century Indian art, art criticism, and aesthetics. At an equally complex level of integration, **A. K. Ramanujan** combined his career as a bilingual writer of poetry and fiction in English and Kannada with his simultaneous careers as a prolific theorist and interpreter of several Indian literatures and cultures, and as a unique twentieth-century literary translator—translating contemporary English materials into Kannada, and translating into English from ancient and modern Tamil and Kannada, as well as (with collaborators) from Sanskrit, Telugu, and Malayalam.

This variety of artistic achievement is not just a contemporary phenomenon. Historically, the modern Indian ideal of versatility goes back at least one hundred and fifty years. Between the last two decades of the nineteenth century and the first four decades of the twentieth, Rabindranath Tagore created the most wide-ranging mixture of this kind, effectively defining the paradigm for future generations: he was a poet, short story writer, novelist, and dramatist, as well as an essayist, critic, autobiographer, travel writer, correspondent, and translator, winning the Nobel Prize for literature in 1913; at the same time, he was also a major lyricist and composer of music, a marvellous painter in his old age, a religious thinker, a nationalist, an antinationalist, a national hero, an orator, a public father-figure, a teacher, a theorist of education, and the founder of a major university in Bengal. Given this sort of range, a systematic account of the social contexts of modern Indian poetry is likely to turn rapidly into a full-scale social and cultural history of nineteenth- and twentieth-century India.

4

The heterogeneity of the social world of modern Indian poetry, however, does not end there. As I suggested earlier, in the post-colonial decades, that world has undergone a new series of far-reaching transformations. For one, during the past thirty years, it has been altered increasingly and with great effect by the emergence of women poets in the various languages. Until the end of the British Raj, and even in the first decade after independence, there were few prominent women poets in the country: in the second half of the nineteenth century, for instance, there was Toru Dutt (English); between the two world wars, there were a handful of figures like Sarojini Naidu (English), and **Mahadevi Varma** and Subhadra Kumari Chauhan (Hindi); and in the final years of colonial rule, there were a few younger women like Indira Sant (Marathi) and Balamani Amma (Malayalam). Since the late 1950s, however, the number of women poets in print has risen sharply. This shift is part of the larger, more dramatic trajectory of change Indian women have been creating for themselves in the domestic and public spheres, especially in the domains of literacy, education, journalism, scholarship, the arts, the entertainment industry, politics, and the various modern professions. Between the 1950s and 1970s, we therefore find women poets like **Amrita Pritam** (Punjabi), Kamala Das (English), and **Nabaneeta Dev Sen** (Bengali) working concurrently with fiction writers like Qurratulain Hyder (Urdu), Anita Desai and Kamala Markandeya (both English), and Mahashweta Devi (Bengali), scholars like Irawati Karve (Marathi) and Romila Thapar and Meenakshi Mukherjee (both English), translators like Lila Ray (Bengali and English), and editors like Madhu Kishwar (English and Hindi) to bring into existence a large, well-defined emergent community of women intellectuals, and a formidable body of women's post-colonial writing in the various languages. In the 1980s there has been virtually an explosion of women's poetry in India, with dozens of new names and voices in English, Marathi, Hindi, Bengali, Oriya, Malayalam, Telugu, Tamil and Kannada—a phenomenon generously represented in these pages, where about half the contributors are younger and older women writers of the post-independence decades.

The situation of women poets in Indian English, in fact, may be a good measure of the change as a whole. In the 1960s the foreground was occupied by relatively isolated figures like Monika Verma and Kamala Das. In the 1970s Gauri Deshpande, Malathi Rao, Anna Sujatha Mathai, Lakshmi Kannan, Mamta Kalia, and Sunita Jain, as well as Eunice de Souza, Melanie Silgardo, Priya Karunaka, Debjani Chatterjee, Nasima Aziz, and **Meena Alexander** entered the picture, giving it the look of a community of women poets. In the 1980s and early 1990s, Imtiaz Dharker, Tilottama Rajan, Charmayne D'Souza, Shanta Acharya, Menka Shivdasani, **Chitra Divakaruni**, and Sujata Bhatt, among others, filled the frame, joining (whether they wanted to or not) the poets who had survived from the previous decades, and giving that community an impressive new profile. Together with their counterparts in the other languages, these women writers have effectively displaced Indian writing from its 'traditional male-dominated centres.'

During the post-colonial decades, the Indian literary world has also been altered by powerful new writers (both men and women) from formerly suppressed or marginal social groups and communities. In the 1960s, and especially in the 1970s, poets from lower-class and lower-caste backgrounds began aggressively and systematically challenging the canons of middle-class and upper-caste literary establishments in languages like Telugu, Kannada, Tamil, and Malayalam, as well as Bengali, Marathi, and Hindi. Many of these 'subaltern' writers came from small towns and communities quite far from the metropolitan centres of Bombay and Calcutta, Delhi and Madras, Lucknow and Hyderabad, writing protest poetry and participating in broader cultural movements in places like Ajmer, Aurangabad, Belgaum, Bhubaneshwar, Ernakulam, Meerut, Nagpur, Patna, and Amravati (where, for example, the Marathi writer **Vasant Abaji Dahake** lives and works). Among the poetic movements that emerged from this wider phenomenon were the Digambara ('naked poetry') movement in Andhra Pradesh, the controversial and short-lived

Hungry Generation movement in Bengal, and the Marxist-Leninist (Naxalite) movement of revolutionary writing in different parts of the country. The best-known movement of this kind, of course, turned out to be the Dalit movement, which began in Maharashtra in the 1950s under the leadership of Dr B. R. Ambedkar, and spread subsequently to neighbouring states like Karnataka as well as to such distant ones as Punjab. The Maharashtrian Dalits are former untouchables from castes like the Mahars, the Mangs, and the Chamars, who have converted to Buddhism in a collective revolt against the institutions and power structures of Hinduism, and have frequently used poetry, fiction, autobiography, and essays as one of their primary means of political action.

As a heterogeneous group of writers from formerly marginal communities, these poets force us to question our most common and far-reaching assumptions about the modern Indian literatures, their social constitution and functions, their canons, aesthetics, and establishments, and their implication in the institutions of power. Converging unexpectedly in the 1970s and 1980s, the women poets and the subaltern poets have broadened and changed the social world of contemporary poetry to an extent we still cannot assess or foresee.

5

The social, literary, and historical contexts discussed in this essay are only selective examples from a broader, more complex range of phenomena that have shaped and reshaped the Indian literatures at the local, regional, and national levels in the course of the nineteenth and twentieth centuries. The historical process has now entered yet one more distinctive phase. In the 1980s, a new generation of writers appeared in print, consisting of men and women who were born after Partition and independence, and whose earliest childhood memories and experiences therefore go back at most to the 1950s. These 'children of *Midnight's Children*' have grown up in a country which is separated by a massive rupture from the India of the Raj, the larger 'India' that writers born before 1947 knew, discovered, portrayed, recovered, freed, changed, and even took for granted. The figures of the new

235

generation who are best known at present—Vikram Seth, Amitav Ghosh, Allan Sealy, Upamanyu Chatterjee, and **Shashi Tharoor** in prose and fiction, and Seth, **Agha Shahid Ali**, **Meena Alexander** and Sujata Bhatt in verse—write in English, publish their work in England and America, and receive generous praise from cosmopolitan international audiences. In the course of the next twenty or thirty years, they and their counterparts in the Indian languages, functioning as both the sites and the instruments of a larger process of change, will once more alter our conceptions of what 'India' is and has been, 'of what is past, or passing, or to come.'

magazines in India. She has also translated Bengali novels into English for Penguin India.

Urmila Banerjee was born in Calcutta and graduated from Wellesley College. Her stories have appeared in *The Bombay Literary Review* and *London Magazine*. She now lives and works in Bombay.

Ram Basu is a Bengali poet who lives in Calcutta.

J. Bernard Bate is a graduate student in anthropology at the University of Chicago. He has studied Tamil for over ten years.

V. Indira Bhavani was born in 1942 in Aruppukkottai, Kamraj District, Tamil Nadu. She uses the pen names Ivara and Indhu Varadan. In addition to her three collections of poems, she has also published a collection of short stories, *Nijangal (Naked Truths)*.

Chandrakanti is the pen name of R. Uma Maheswari, who was born in 1961 in Edapet, South Arcot District, Tamil Nadu. She has published two collections of poems and short stories in leading Tamil magazines. She is from an agricultural family of Edapet village.

Gita Chattopadhyay was born in 1941 into a traditional landholding family in North Calcutta, where she continues to live with her family. She has published three volumes of poetry and verse drama to date, and one critical work. Her recent poems have appeared in the magazines, *Kabi O Kabita* and *Samved*.

Vijay Chauhan (1931–1988) wrote short stories in Hindi and lived in the US from the 1970s on. He grew up in Jabalpur, studied in Delhi, and taught at Sagar (Madhya Pradesh). He published two collections of stories, *Mizraab* (1972) and *Ekantvas* (1989).

Ajeet Cour, a Punjabi writer and journalist, has written twelve books. The first part of her autobiography, *The Nomad*, won the Sahitya Akademi Award in 1986. Her stories are regularly featured on radio and television, and have been translated into several languages.

Vasant Abaji Dahake has published two collections of poems, as well as several short stories and novellas. He teaches Marathi literature at Elphinstone College, Bombay.

B. K. Das teaches at the National University of Singapore.

Jagannath Prasad Das was born in 1936 in Bhubaneswar, Orissa.

He is an accomplished writer in many genres, including poetry, fiction, drama, and art history.

Nabaneeta Dev Sen was born in 1938 in Calcutta, the only child of Bengali poets Narendra Dev and Radharani Devi. She received a Ph.D. in comparative literature from Indiana University. She has published four novels, two collections of short fiction, three travelogues, two collections of verse, and two critical studies. She is professor of comparative literature at Jadavpur University in Calcutta.

Aparna Dharwadker teaches drama, Restoration, and Eighteenth-century British literature in the Department of English, University of Oklahoma. She has published translations of modern poetry and prose from Hindi.

Vinay Dharwadker teaches in the English department at the University of Oklahoma. His published work includes poems, translations from Hindi and Marathi, literary essays, reviews, and scholarly articles. He has edited (with A. K. Ramanujan) *Modern Indian Poetry: An Anthology* (forthcoming from Oxford University Press and University of California Press). His first collection of poems titled *Sunday at the Lodi Gardens* was published by Penguin India in 1994.

Aruna Dhere was born in Pune in 1957. She started writing when she was ten, and has three collections of Marathi poetry to her credit.

Chitra Divakaruni was born in India and now lives in the San Francisco Bay area, where she teaches English and creative writing at Foothill College. Her works have appeared in *The Beloit Poetry Journal, The Threepenny Review, Chelsea, Colorado Review*, and *Indiana Review*. She has written three books of poetry: *Dark Like the River, The Reason for Nasturtiums*, and *Black Candle*.

Ketaki Kushari Dyson was born in West Bengal in 1939. Educated in Calcutta and Oxford, she is a longtime resident of Kidlington, England. She has published poetry, novels, and criticism in both Bengali and English.

Born in 1938 in Bangladesh, **Sunil Gangopadhyay** has written numerous novels and short stories on Bengali life, including the historic *Sei Samay*. He works for the Ananda Bazaar Patrika Group of pubiications, Calcutta.

Gagan Gill was born in 1959 in New Delhi. She published her first collection of poems in 1989. In 1990, she attended the International Writing Program at the University of Iowa. She is the Hindi editor of *The Telegraph* in Delhi.

Teji Grover, born in 1955 in Pathankot, Punjab, teaches in the Department of English in MCM Dayanand Anglo-Vedic College in Chandigarh. She has published two collections of poetry in Hindi.

Popati Hiranandani was born in 1924 in Hyderabad, Sind. She was educated at Benares Hindu University. Devoted to the recognition of Sindhi language and literature, she has published forty-five books. She won the Sahitya Akademi Award in 1982.

Vinda Karandikar was born in 1918 and taught English in Bombay for more than thirty years. He was the most prominent "new poet" to appear in Marathi soon after independence. He has been an influential critic, translator, and theoretician of literature in Marathi and English. He wrote "Himayoga" during and after a year as a Senior Fulbright Fellow at the University of Chicago in 1967–68.

Born in 1932, **Arun Kolatkar** became famous in the 1960s as one of the avant garde poets of Bombay, writing poetry in both English and Marathi. His only volume of poems in English, *Jejuri* (1977), won the Commonwealth Poetry Prize in English, and his collected poems in Marathi, *Arun Kolatkarchya Kavita* (1978), won the Maharashtra State award. He has worked in advertising for nearly three decades.

Jayanta Mahapatra is a widely published poet. His recent publications include *Selected Poems* (Oxford, 1987), *Burden of Waves and Fruit* (Three Continents, 1988), *Temple* (Dangaroo, 1989) and *The Whiteness of Bone* (Penguin India, 1992). His work appears regularly in magazines such as the *Hudson Review*, *Kenyon Review*, and *Poetry*.

Sitakanta Mahapatra was born in 1937 and attended Utkal, Allahabad, and Cambridge Universities. A major Indian poet, he has published ten anthologies of poems in Oriya and seven in English translation. His poetry has been translated into all the Indian languages, as well as six European languages. He has translated and edited eight anthologies of the oral poetry of the Indian tribes. He was the recipient of the Jnanpith award in 1993.

Mala Marwah was born in District Sarguja (Madhya Pradesh) and educated at the Universities of Delhi and Baroda. She is a painter, poet, and writer on contemporary Indian painting. She is also a well-known translator.

R. Meenakshi was born in 1947 in Virudhunagar, Tamil Nadu. A poet, teacher, and social worker, she has been an educational researcher since 1976 in Auroville, the international township founded by 'The Mother' of the Sri Aurobindo Ashram. She has published four collections of poetry.

Leslie Minot studies comparative literature (Bengali) in the graduate program at the University of California (Berkeley).

Kanchan Kuntala Mukherjee was born in Calcutta in 1953. She holds a Ph.D. in modern Bengali poetry. She has published three books of poetry and translated the *Gita Govinda* from Sanskrit to Bengali. She has written poetry and essays for a variety of magazines.

Asha Mundlay was born in Pune in 1936. She is an anthropologist, linguist, and feminist theorist and teaches Marathi.

C. M. Naim teaches Urdu literature in the Department of South Asian Languages and Civilisations at the University of Chicago.

Rukmini Bhaya Nair studied at Calcutta and Cambridge, where she received her doctorate in linguistics in 1982. Her collection of poems, *The Hyoid Bone*, was published by Penguin India in 1993, and a work on narrative theory called *Narrative Norms, Conversational Conventions* is forthcoming as well. She teaches at the Jawaharlal Nehru University, Delhi at the Centre of Linguistics and English.

Pratibha Nandkumar, author of three volumes of poetry in Kannada and numerous articles, lives in Bangalore.

Nara (V. Narayana Rao) is a literary critic and translator of Telugu. He teaches at the University of Wisconsin, Madison. He was a Guggenheim Fellow in 1991–92.

Kunwar Narayan was born in 1926 and has spent most of his life in Lucknow, where he runs an automobile business. His early short and long poems were characterized as obscure and experimental, and had a strong impact on new Hindi poetry after the 1950s.

Mrinal Pande was born in Nainital in 1946. She is well-known as a playwright and fiction writer in Hindi. She was the editor of *Vama*, a *Times of India* Hindi monthly for women from 1981–87, and is currently editor of *The Hindustan Times* weekly, *Saptahik Hindustan*. Her collection of short stories, *Daughter's Daughter* was published by Penguin India in 1993.

Ayyappa Paniker was born in Kerala in 1930. He received a Ph.D. from Indiana, and now teaches at the Institute of English at the University of Kerala, Trivandrum. He edits *Medieval Indian Literature* for the Sahitya Akademi, and is an award-winning poet in Malayalam.

K. Paramasivam (1933–1992) was born in Viravanallur, Tirunelveli District, Tamil Nadu. An accomplished linguist, he lived in Madurai and directed the American Institute of Indian Studies Tamil Language Program from 1986 until his death in January 1992. He taught at American College, Madurai, for thirty years, and translated more than twenty English classics into Tamil. He held a Ph. D. in linguistics from the University of Chicago.

Harishankar Parsai, the foremost satirist in Hindi, has been a prolific writer of essays, stories, and newspaper columns for four decades. Some of these have been collected in six volumes. He lives in Jabalpur (Madhya Pradesh).

R. Parthasarathy is the author of the long poem *Rough Passage* (4th printing, Oxford, 1989), and has edited *Ten Twentieth-Century Indian Poets* (11th Printing, Oxford, 1990). He has translated into modern English verse the celebrated Tamil classic, *Shilappadikaram* (5th century CE; *The Epic of the Anklet*, Columbia, 1993). His poems and translations have appeared in *Chelsea*, *London Magazine*, *Salmagundi*, and *The Times Literary Supplement*. He teaches English and Asian Studies at Skidmore College.

Gieve Patel has published three collections of verse as well as three plays. He is a general medical practitioner with a private clinic in Bombay. In 1989, he was awarded a Woodrow Wilson Fellowship for his work in the theatre.

Karamshi Pir has been translating creative and critical prose from all over the world into Gujarati for three decades. He lives in Bombay and prefers to do nothing for a living.

Surendra Prakash, born in 1930 in Lyallpur, West Punjab (now part of Pakistan), has published three volumes of short stories, and is currently working on a novel, *Fassaan*. He lives in Bombay and writes for the movies.

Amrita Pritam was born in Punjab in 1919. She has published almost fifty books, and won the Sahitya Akademi Award in 1956. Since 1966 she has edited the journal *Nagamani*. In 1966, *Mahfil (The Journal of South Asian Literature)* devoted an issue to her work. A former Member of Parliament, she now lives in Delhi.

Born in Kerala in 1955, Savitri Rajeevan has been published in many anthologies and is a regular contributor to Malayalam periodicals. She works with the journal *Samskar Keralam*, and lives in Trivandrum.

Sundara Ramaswami was born in 1931 and lives in Nagercoil. Ramaswami edits the literary journal *Kalaccuvatu*, and has published several volumes of short stories and two novels in Tamil.

A. K. Ramanujan was a poet—he published four volumes in English, three in Kannada—and translator of Kannada and Tamil literature. His translations include *Speaking of Siva* (1973), *Hyms for the Drowning* (1981) and *Poems of Love and War* (1986). His *Folktales From India* was published by Penguin India in 1993. He died in Chicago in October 1993.

Ramakanta Rath joined the Indian Administrative Service in 1957. He began writing while in college and has published six anthologies of poems. He lives in New Delhi.

Satyajit Ray (1921–1992) was awarded the Oscar for Lifetime Achievement and the Bharat Ratna in 1992. He not only wrote the screenplays and directed more than 50 films, but also cast the parts, designed the costumes, scored music, edited and sketched the promotional material for his films. He also published a number of books which include *Adventures of Feluda* (1988), *20 Stories* (1992) and *Further Adventures of Feluda* (1993) with Penguin India.

Since retiring from the Indian Administrative Service, Sunil B. Ray has translated extensively from French, Spanish, and Persian into Bengali and from Bengali into French and English. His work has appeared in many Bengali magazines, including *Anubad Patrika* and *Jugantar*.

P. S. Rege (1910–1978) studied economics in Bombay and London, and made his career as a teacher and educator. He was one of the new "modernist" poets in Marathi in the late 1930s and 1940s, and published poetry, fiction, and essays regularly for over five decades.

Raghuvir Sahay (1929–1990) was a poet, journalist and editor who lived in Lucknow and New Delhi. He published poetry, short fiction, literary criticism, and social and political essays, and also successfully translated Shakespeare's *Macbeth* and *Othello* for the Hindi stage.

Vilas Sarang holds a Ph. D. from both Bombay and Indiana Universities. He teaches English at the University of Bombay. His short stories appeared widely in various magazines, and in a collection, *Fair Tree of the Void* (Penguin India, 1990).

Aditi Nath Sarkar was formerly associated with the University of Chicago and the University of Minnesota. He now resides in India, where he works as a translator and also makes films.

Martha Ann Selby was born in 1954 in Nevada, Iowa. A former Fulbright scholar, she received her doctorate from the Department of South Asian Languages and Civilizations, the University of Chicago. She has published articles on Old Tamil, Sanskrit, and Prakrit poetry as well as numerous translations. She teaches at Southern Methodist University.

Satadru Sen is a graduate student at the University of California (Berkeley) in South Asian studies. He writes poetry and short fiction.

B. C. Ramachandra Sharma, born in 1925, emerged as one of the leaders of modernism in Kannada during the 1950s. Well-known for his poetry, short stories, and plays, he has also edited a volume of Kannada short stories for Penguin India titled *Modern Kannada Short Stories*.

Gulam mohammed Sheikh was born in 1937 at Surendranagar in Saurashtra (Gujarat). He trained as a painter in Baroda and London, and has had several exhibitions in India and elsewhere, including a retrospective, 'Returning Home', at the Centre Georges Pompidou, Paris, in 1985. His poetry and prose writings have appeared widely in Gujarati journals and in several major anthologies. He is professor of painting at the University of Baroda.

Prayag Shukla was born in Calcutta in 1940, and was educated at Calcutta University. He has published collections of his poetry, short stories, and art criticism. He also served on the editorial board of the Hindi literary magazine, *Dinman*.

Kedarnath Singh was born in Ballia District (Uttar Pradesh) in 1934. He received his Ph. D. from Banaras Hindu University, and has taught Hindi at Jawaharlal Nehru University since 1978. He has published three volumes of poetry and two critical studies. Since the late 1950s, he has been associated with "the new poetry" and the "progressive" writers' movement in Hindi.

Krishna Sobti, born in 1925 in Gujrat, West Punjab (now in Pakistan), was educated in Delhi, Simla, and Lahore. Her writing shows a deep familiarity with Punjabi idiom and style, and a wide-ranging exploration of female experience. She has published six novels and several collections of short fiction and essays. She won the Sahitya Akademi Award in 1980 for her novel, *Zindaginama* (*Chronicle of a Life*).

Shashi Tharoor was born in London in 1956 and grew up in Bombay and Calcutta. He holds a Ph. D. from the Fletcher School of Law and Diplomacy at Tufts University. He has worked at the United Nations since 1978, serving eleven years with the U. N. High Commissioner for Refugees. Among his many publications are *The Great Indian Novel* (1989), *The Five-Dollar Smile and Other Stories* (1991) and *Show Business* which was published by Penguin India and Arcade/Little, Brown in 1991 and 1992 respectively.

Sunanda Tripathy is one of Orissa's youngest women poets. She works as a journalist in Puri.

Harish Trivedi teaches English at the University of Delhi. He has translated *Premchand: His Life and Times* (1982; reprinted Oxford, 1991), and has published a book on the mutual interaction between English literature and Indian literature.

S. Usha writes her poetry in Kannada.

Krishna Baldev Vaid has published over twenty books in Hindi, including seven novels, eight collections of stories, and several translations. His books in English include *Steps in Darkness* (Orion), *Bimal in Bog* (Writers Workshop) and *Dying Alone* (Penguin India). His latest novel titled, *Broken Mirror* will be published by Penguin India in 1994.

Mahadevi Varma (1907–1986), recipient of the nation's highest literary honour, the Jnanpith award, is celebrated for her contributions to Romantic poetry. She is also known for *Shrinkhala Ki Kadiyan* (*The Links of Our Chains*), a collection of feminist essays published between 1931 and 1937, from which "The Art of Living" is excerpted.

H. S. Venkateshamurthy was born in 1944 and resides in Bangalore. He is the author of eight volumes of poetry in Kannada, and has translated the works of Kalidasa.

Kamal Vora has been writing poetry for the last two decades. His poems have appeared in leading Gujarati journals and his first collection, *Arav* (*Silence*), was published in 1991. He lives in Bombay and works as an engineer in his own business.

Carolyne Wright visited Calcutta on a 1986–88 Indo-American Fellowship, to study and translate, with the assistance of native-speaking collaborators, the work of Bengali women poets and writers. Her translations have appeared in numerous journals in the US, and she has published four collections of her own work. She recently completed a Fulbright in Bangladesh and a Bunting Fellowship at Radcliffe.

Arlene R. K. Zide received her Ph. D. in linguistics and South Asian languages from the University of Chicago. She teaches at Washington College in Chicago. She is herself a poet, and on a recent Fulbright to India collected and translated poetry for an anthology, *In Their Own Voice: The Penguin Anthology of Contemporary Indian Women Poets*, published by Penguin India in 1993.

MORE ABOUT PENGUINS

For further information about books available from Penguins in India write to Penguin Books (India) Ltd, 210 Chiranjiv Tower 43, Nehru Place, New Delhi 110 019.

In the UK: For a complete list of books available from Penguins in the United Kingdom write to Dept. EP, Penguin Books Ltd, Harmondsworth, Middlesex UB7 0DA.

In the U.S.A.: For a complete list of books available from Penguins in the United States write to Dept. DG, Penguin Books, 299 Murray Hill Parkway, East Rutherford, New Jersey 07073.

In Canada: For a complete list of books available from Penguins in Canada write to Penguin Books Canada Ltd, 2801 John Street, Markham, Ontario L3R 1B4.

In Australia: For a complete list of books available from Penguins in Australia write to the Marketing Department, Penguin Books Australia Ltd, P.O. Box 257, Ringwood, Victoria 3134.

In New Zealand: For a complete list of books available from Penguins in New Zealand write to the Marketing Department, Penguin Books (N.Z.) Ltd, Private Bag, Takapuna, Auckland 9.

FROM CAUVERY TO GODAVARI
Modern Kannada Short Stories
Edited by Ramachandra Sharma

This is a collection of fifteen masterly stories from Karnataka's long and outstanding story-telling tradition and brings together the work of S. Diwakar, D. Mahadeva, Vaidehi and K.R. Anantha Murthy among other exemplars of the modern short fiction. Ramachandra Sharma's short story, *The Passage*, sets the ball rolling.

Most of the stories in this collection are indeed powerful and even the literality that creeps up in translation does not reduce their impact

—*Suchitra Behal*

THE COLOUR OF NOTHINGNESS
Modern Urdu Short Stories
Edited by M.U. Memon

Here are samples from one of the subcontinent's richest literary genres—the Urdu short story. From Zamiruddin Ahmad's 'Sukhe Sawan' to Sharwan Kumar Verma's 'Deep as the Ocean' there are sixteen stories that dazzle with their wit, brilliance and intelligence.

These stories are often macabre, surreal; a quick flash of vivid images that barely gives you a chance to put them together in your head to form a whole. All the stories, however, have in common the overwhelming centrality of mood . . . the quality of being haunted by other times and past promises . . .

Githa Hariharan in Deccan Herald

FOR THE BEST IN PAPERBACKS, LOOK FOR THE ⦵

THE GOLDEN WAIST CHAIN
Modern Hindi Short Stories
Edited by Sara Rai

A selection of some of the best Hindi stories of the last forty years, this collection is a representative volume of the *Nai Kahani* genre and includes the work of Nirmal Varma, Muktibodh and Mohan Rakesh among others. Sara Rai's translation skills couple with her heritage for she is Premchand's granddaughter.

Such collections would be welcome for fiction from other Indian languages as well

—*Makarand Paranjape in Femina.*

THE PENGUIN BOOK OF MODERN INDIAN
SHORT STORIES
Edited by Stephen Alter & Wimal Dissanayake

This collection has eighteen stories by Bharati Mukherjee, Anita Dasai and Bhisham Sahni among others, some of them anthologized elsewhere to great acclaim. All of them have been written in the last fifty years and combined in a rich spectrum of pleasures that this popular genre has typically provided—especially in the hands of masters writing in over a dozen languages of the subcontinent.

As a glimpse into the nuts and bolts of the Indian middle class . . . the stories are invigorating vignettes.

—*Subhash K Jha*

Another myth that this selection succeeds in exploding is that Indian writing rests on a few giants like Tagore and Premchand. The reader needed to be introduced to 'modern' writing.

—*Financial Express.*

GREY PIGEON AND OTHER STORIES
Neelam Saran Gour

Gour's collection of short stories confirms her growing reputation as a fine writer of fiction. Her style is refreshingly un-self-conscious such that the academic distinction between style and storyline is obviated. Characters as colourful as the parts of India where they belong are to be found as each story unfolds; the camaraderie that exists between a four-year-old and his Nana in 'Song of Innocence and Experience', a senile but lovable Nawab finds people still retain old values in these changed times in 'The Taste of Almonds.'

Each story in this collection illuminates a particular universe, completely authentic in texture and detail . . .

Ritu Menon in Indian Review of Books.